JUST DOGS

HIS CUE

JUST DOGS

Sketches in

PEN & PENCIL

by

K. F. BARKER

LONDON: COUNTRY LIFE LTD

NEW YORK: CHARLES SCRIBNER'S SONS

First Published in October 1933
Reprinted November 1933
Reprinted January 1934
Reprinted October 1934
Popular Edition October 1935
Reprinted July 1936
Reprinted October 1937

PRINTED IN GREAT BRITAIN

Introduction

*   *

IT is, I believe, fairly common in an introduction to a book, to take the opportunity of making some kind of apology for the book itself, giving at length the various reasons which caused the author to commit the crime of writing it, and pleading for the clemency and understanding of those people who, he fears, but at the same time secretly and fondly hopes, will read it.

As I, however, have no pretensions to being an author—a fact which will at once be apparent to those who read these random scribblings by one to whom the pen is much less familiar than the pencil—it is perhaps scarcely necessary for me to make excuses, but at the same time a word or two in extenuation may not be out of place.

The drawings in the book, which in many cases have no reference to the letterpress facing them, have been selected at random from my sketch-books, and are merely notes and memories, ' snap-shots ' of my dog ' pals ' and acquaintances which I have jotted down in pen and pencil in all sorts of places, and in varying moods ; hence the absence of any attempt to maintain a certain level or sequence in either sketches or letterpress, neither of which pretends to be anything more than impressions and memories.

This brings me to the somewhat conspicuous absence of ' points ' in the dogs which figure in the drawings. I can only say that the majority of the dogs of my acquaintance are very far from being good dogs in the eyes of the stickler for show points, they are merely ' dogs ', and can only be judged as such ; not on their possession of wonderful ' fronts ' and perfect proportions, but on their more lasting and loveable qualities of heart and brain, which endure to the end, long after such poor vanities as ' coats ' and ' ear carriage ' have ceased to count.

I must reluctantly confess, then, that the majority of my dog friends portrayed here are, alas, only the ordinary children of ordinary parents ; in fact some few among them fail to reach even this standard, but, being the care-free result of some light-hearted and fantastic *mésalliance*, remain Just Dogs.

v

And how attractive some of these cross-breds are ! I can remember one in particular ; it was at a lonely little farm in Yorkshire ; he was a cream-coloured, shaggy fellow with a long tail and very fierce, light eyes, rather on the lines of that ancient and valued breed the Border sheep-dog. Patting the dog's head, and more for something to say than for any other reason, I asked the little girl at the farm what sort of a dog her pet was.

She drew herself up proudly and replied :

' He's a pure-bred mongreel '.

I liked her pronunciation of the last word, it sounded so much nicer than mongrel, which is always rather offensive to the ear.

Perhaps the reason why I cherish a particular dislike to the word, is because I am the possessor of a dog who does not happen to be a mongrel, but who looks exactly like one.

He figures as the frontispiece of this book and in "Watch Me ! " (p. 12), and most people when they discover that he is not a mongrel are disappointed, and just a little hurt. When I explain to them that he really and truly does possess a mother and a father both of the same breed they say rather discontentedly, ' Oh, *really* ', and then more cheerfully, ' But you know he'd pass for a mongrel *anywhere* ' !

Upon which I delve deeply into the past in search of confirmatory evidence of the blameless respectability of my dog's parents, and such is the obstinate disbelief of some of these people that, short of producing his mother's marriage lines, I often despair of establishing the right of my dog to a breed at all !

It is astonishing the pains we take to defend the ' points ' of our dogs, and if, as is sometimes unfortunately the case, the said points are too glaringly non-existent, how easily and gracefully we fall back on some outstanding virtue in the dog's character, or some engaging little way that he has, and dangle this in front of our critics.

This hot-headed defence on our part is quite natural and just as it should be, because our dogs are worthy of it, they are so much better and more likeable in every way than the ordinary sorts belonging to other people, cleaner, better looking, more intelligent and so forth. In fact these dogs of ours become so much a part of us, that we can no longer view them with a cool impartial eye ; they are the kindly mirrors in which we invariably see ourselves, not as we really are, but as we should all like to be. And what splendid people we should be if only we were really the magnificent creatures they think us.

To them we are God-like, in their generous eyes can do no wrong; and most of us do so pitifully little to attain this wonderful pedestal. Our sins of omission and commission, and particularly the former, are legion, and yet how rarely, even though we have fulfilled only a tiny part of our share of the bond, do they 'let us down'. If we are any sort of a dog owner at all, we can bank on our dog to the end. And the more roughly they are treated the closer do they stand by.

Talking of dogs standing by recalls to my mind a little story of an old Irish sportsman who used, by invitation, to hunt a pack of otter-hounds in County Cork. His appearance at the meet always caused any strangers who happened to be present intense amusement, when they saw coming round the corner a little flat cart drawn by a very fat pony whose harness consisted of a complicated arrangement of rope and string. Solemnly seated on the cart were six enormous foxhounds, and walking alongside, pole in hand, would be the old sportsman who always insisted on bringing his six hounds with him.

The day's sport over the old man would retire to the nearest inn (never very far from the meet) and drink steadily. In due course he would be carried out by his friends and carefully placed on the little flat cart, with a few armfuls of hay and a bundle of the same for a pillow; the huge hounds would take their places three on either side of the cart, the old pony would be started up and the procession would journey thus the seven miles to the old man's home.

A friend of mine who was out with these hounds asked the question, ' What are the police about to allow the old man to return from his day's sport, and drive about the country in such a condition ? '

There was a laugh of derision :

' Arrah ! an is ut thim blagguards av police that would be afther raisin' a finger ? Don't they well know that anny one o' thim hounds of Mickey's would have the throats of thim tore out if they shtopped him on the road ! '

And there would seem to be some truth in this, as a single constable, cycling along the road, the moment he sighted the strange equipage, jumped off, and pulling his machine up the bank side ' viewed the landscape o'er ' until the sleeping Mickey and his formidable guardians had passed. Mickey's faith in his rather savage guards was evidently justified, as not a policeman in the district ever ventured to pull him up.

The material in this book, both pen and pencil sketches—with two exceptions—deals entirely with dogs who are ' all present ' and very much alive, but I would like to add a parting word, and call a toast to those of our dog ' pals ' who've gone over the hill ; my toast to them is " Happy Days ! "

I like to think that all those dogs who have had a ' thin ' time on earth will, in a heaven of their own, receive in large measure all those joys which were denied them here.

It pleases me to imagine all those countless little terriers whose good looks made of their lives a burden, and who were dragged from show to show, who have never known the joys of chasing the elusive ' cotton tail ' through the thick undergrowth and never ' pinned ' a rat, doing in their particular paradise all these things, and fulfilling the purpose for which God gave them a sensitive nose, four active legs, and an eager spirit.

And just think what a glorious time those ' sheltered ' dogs may have, who here on earth were never allowed out ' off the lead ', and were never, never permitted to fight another dog, play in the mud, or roll in dirt. Their lives perhaps will be just one long series of fights, mud, and lovely strong smells—and chains and leads will be things unknown. And surely, for every hour of martyrdom a dog spends on earth anchored to a small wooden cage, he will in heaven receive seven-fold hours of perfect freedom, and acres of green turf to gallop over with the breezes blowing past his ears.

And I hope we shan't, and somehow I don't think we shall, see Alsatians there as we see them here, pacing the crowded streets on short chains and ' choke ' collars ; no, surely they will be stretching those lithe limbs of theirs in swift, smooth motion—living poems of movement—and ' choke ' collars will be things unknown.

And all the old hounds I think will be young again, rousing the echoes with their wild joyous crash of music as once again they're ' on the line ', hunting the elusive otter to his ' holt ' in some dark and

viii

secret pool ; spreading out over the heather in tireless pursuit of a royal stag, and fleeting over the grass on the scent of a game red fox, who, of course, heaven being heaven, would have no objection to being chased.

I suppose we all of us at some time cherish some dim idea of heaven as we hope it will be to each one of us ; mine I know will not be complete unless that little band of ' dear acquaintances ' are at the gate to meet me, and tell me of all the best walks, where the rabbits are, and all the most promising holes which shelter the shy water rats, so that we may share again all those joyous adventures which we enjoyed together on earth.

And so to that goodly company who have gone on before, I say again, " Happy Days ! "

K. F. BARKER

Contents

★   ★

	PAGE
INTRODUCTION	V
THE OTHER FELLOW'S PLACE	1
WANTED—A CONVENIENT DOG	4
GIVE A DOG A BAD NAME	7
IT WAS A FAMOUS VICTORY	10
HIS PROPER PLACE	15
THE BRUISER	19
DOGS ON LEADS	21
ROY THE RANGER	23
THE DOG'S MENU	25
DAVID AND JONATHAN	27
PADDY—PORTRAIT OF A LADY	29
SPOTS	32
THE UNINVITED GUEST	35
TIME, GENTLEMEN!	37
HIS FIRST FLEA	42
CHANGING BEDS	45
THE STOP-GAP	47
A COUPLE OF RABBITS	49
THE HORSE-COPER'S LURCHER	52
PATRICK	56
HOUNDS ARE OUT	58
WALKS	60
THE PENSIONER	61
THE LAST WORD	63
OTHER PEOPLE'S DOGS	66
BORROWED PLUMES	68
THE BEST DOG OF ALL	71

THE SUPPLIANT

Where did you get that coat, Mister ?

List of Sketches

★　　★

HIS CUE

THE SUPPLIANT

'WHERE DID YOU GET THAT COAT, MISTER?'

AN OBJECT TO MAKE THE HACKLES OF ALL SELF-RESPECTING DOGS
      BRISTLE WITH HORROR

PLACED IN THE FAR CORNER OF THE LITTLE YARD AT THE BACK

'I'M SICK OF WOMEN'

THE TWINS

MOODS OF 'MAC'

MOODS OF 'MAC'

THE INCORRUPTIBLE

'I COULD HAVE MY CHAIR IF I COULD TALK FRENCH!'

'WATCH ME!'

RUMPUS AT THE SHOW

MISSED!

THE EGOIST

A-HUNTING WE WILL GO!

LITTLE FAT BADGER AND TIM HAVE A DAY OFF

'HI! YOU'RE IN MY BED'

A CUCKOO IN THE NEST

EYE

THE BRUISER—AN IMPRESSION

TIRED

TINKER AND HIS PALS

BLINKERS GOES WALKING

STILL THE SAME OLD ROY THE RANGER

'WE'VE GOT A RABBIT, BUT I DID MOST OF IT'

'JERRY' (IN MEMORY)

THE NATURALIST

CONFABULATION

JUBILATION!

DAVID AND JONATHAN

'EXCUSE ME BUT I'M AFRAID I MUST BE GOING NOW'

'I CHOSE THE LARGEST BED'

'ME, PADDY'

'WHERE ARE THOSE RATSANDRABBITS?'

THE WHITE HOPE

WHO GOES ?
THE FLY
TAILPIECE
'LU WIND 'IM, LADS, LU WIND 'IM !'
KENDAL AND DISTRICT OTTERHOUNDS
'PLEASE, I'VE COME !'
THE UNKNOWN QUANTITY
'MAGPIE' OF THE THREE HARROWS
CAUTIOUS OVERTURES
'A POOR THING BUT MINE OWN'
MISUNDERSTOOD
'OH FOR THE WINGS OF A DOVE'
RIMA FETCHES THE HANDKERCHIEF
'THERE'S SOMETHING WRONG WITH THIS BED !'
'PLEASE, ARE YOU MY DADDY ?'
CAVE !
'CAN'T YOU COME OUT ?'
SLUMBER
FAITH, HOPE AND CHARITY
'THE BLACK BITCH DIDN'T TURN HER HEAD, BUT CONTINUED TO
    SURVEY THE WIDE LONELY STRETCHES OF HEATHER'
'HIS EYES AS THEY RANGED THE NOISY CROWD WERE SAD'
'HOUNDS, PLEASE !'
MATERNAL REFLECTIONS
WORDS
'CHORISTER' SINGING
PATRICK, ANGEL OR DEVIL
'SOMEONE IS CALLING ME, BUT I'M NOT GOING'
THE OLD BEAGLE
TRY OVER, TRY OVER !
PULL DEVIL, PULL BAKER !
OTTER HUNTING
SHE KEPT HER SMALL BRISTLING FORM EFFECTIVELY SCREENED
    FROM THATCHER'S EYE
TAILPIECE
DINNER-TIME
A PUPPY WITH A PAST
THE WEATHEREYE
SAM THE SORROWFUL
'SOME THERE ARE WHO ONLY STAND AND WAIT'
'I'VE HAD MY FUN ANYWAY !'
THAT PUP
'HAVEN'T YOU FINISHED YET ?'

JUST DOGS

The Other Fellow's Place

★   ★

IF people would give that consideration to the selection of their dogs which they bestow on their dress, dinners and wall-papers, there would be far fewer round pegs in square holes. We should then be spared such painful spectacles as the alert, active whippet gradually deteriorating under the ownership of a sweet, old lady, and lapsing into a position it was never intended by nature to occupy—that of a pampered indoor dog. Why, we wonder, cannot the old lady adopt the dog which was, surely, expressly created for her by a kindly and far-seeing Providence? Of course we mean the pug; the round peg in the round hole in his proper sphere, my lady's boudoir.

And why, oh why, is the unfortunate ' Peke ' so frequently chosen for a nursery pet? The little fellow from earliest times was bred with bowed legs for the express purpose of preventing his walking far; in the words of the Mandarins of Peking in their Standard of Points, ' His legs shall be bowed so that he shall not stray from the precincts of the palace '. And yet, how often do we see an unfortunate dog of China hitched to that instrument of dog torture, the baby's ' pram ', and dragged out for his daily martyrdom?

There are quite enough breeds of dogs to-day to suit every kind of person; and, while the selection of certain dogs by totally unsuitable people may cause a good deal of fun for the onlooker, it may be quite the reverse for the dogs so chosen.

The main question to ask yourself when selecting your dog is, can I give this fellow what he requires and has a right to expect? If we live in a town in a small house without a garden, then we know that the Irish wolfhound, Great Dane and bloodhound are not for us, neither are the collie, retriever, nor larger spaniels. We must turn instead to that big company of Die Hards, the small terriers, fox, Welsh, Scotch, Sealyham, etc. A better selection still, if we live far from green fields and country walks, would be a French bulldog, a truly ideal ' pal ' to live with in a town house; clean, short of coat, intelligent, easily trained and a ' one-man sort '.

1

All the terrier tribe must have plenty of exercise, partly because it is a necessity to the breed but also because it helps to keep their volatile spirits more under control. An uncontrolled fox terrier in good spirits can become a curse, not only to his owner but to an entire neighbourhood. Such a dog stands a very good chance of a dose of poison ; a cowardly but not uncommon revenge, and one which often, unfortunately, claims the wrong dog for its victim.

If your choice should be one of the terrier variety, see that you get him young, before he has had time to form any early bad habits. Terriers, be it noted, are inveterate hunters and killers, and require very careful training, and unless kept under good control will almost certainly sooner or later get their owners into trouble. Everything is fish that comes to the terrier's net, whether it be sheep, cats, poultry or errand boys and motor cars. The fox terrier, as a rule, is the worst offender in this respect ; his Scottish and Welsh cousins are all much easier to train, and in some ways make more desirable companions. But, if you are prepared to give up a good deal of time to the training and exercising of your dog, a wire fox terrier takes some beating. He is known, and rightly so, as the Gentleman of the Fancy, and is, I think, easily the best-looking of the terrier family.

Another fairly recent recruit to the ranks of the sporting terriers is the little gentleman from Westmorland, that country of great sportsmen and good dogs ; I mean the Lakeland terrier. Bred originally from some of the gamest breeds in the world, including the Border and Bedlington, he is a real varminty sort, though, as might be expected from his breeding, inclined to be a trifle short in temper. But to fox and otter and for an all-round sporting dog of a handy size this little chap is hard to beat. Again, environment must decide for us, but remember he is, first and foremost and every time, a sporting dog. If intended for the children do not get a Lakeland ; his temper is, as I remarked, a bit gingery and he will not stand for a lot of petting even from his owner.

If the terriers do not appeal, the ever popular little cocker does not make at all a bad ' pal dog '. Very good-natured as a rule, and clean about the house, he is not noisy and in that particular respect he has a decided pull over our friends the terriers. The main thing to guard

2

against in spaniels is their habit of putting on weight ; they are greedy feeders and are also very fond of the fireside, two tastes which probably account for this rather irritating propensity.

If we live in the country and own wide acres, then there is practically no limit to our choice of dogs, from Irish wolfhounds downwards. Some of the larger breeds take more rearing than others, bloodhounds, for instance, being very delicate. All the big-boned, loose-limbed dogs require very careful feeding and exercising if they are to develop on right lines.

Choosing a dog can be a very delightful task, but, once more, before deciding on the favoured breed ' put yourself in the other fellow's place '.

Wanted—A Convenient Dog

★   ★

IT gives me a feeling of irritation when I hear certain people say that they are ' thinking of getting a dog '.

You know the people I mean ; very often a recently married couple after they have achieved the ' home ' complete with every modern convenience, electric fires, ditto cooker, etc., etc., suddenly realise that their up-to-date villa is still short of one more necessary fitment, viz. a dog. They don't want a companion to sit with them in their ' home ', nor yet a ' pal ' to bear them company on their walks ; no, no, that's not what they're after at all.

All they require is a piece of mechanism, on four legs, covered with long or short hair—the latter for preference ; it is more ' convenient '. Colour ? Immaterial but—stay—not all white ; they get so dirty. Sex ? Oh, well, a dog of course ; they are more ' convenient '. Breed ? Oh, something smallish ; big ones get in the way so. And so in the fullness of time they ' get a dog '.

And having provided him with a nice, bright, new, shining chain, the other end of which they attach to a small kennel (this, by the way, need not be built on modern lines) placed in the far corner of the little yard at the back, they fold their hands complacently, firmly convinced that they have amply and generously provided for that dog's welfare. His happiness ? Oh well, he always gets out every day when Baby goes out. He does—tied to the ' pram '—an object to make the hackles of all self-respecting dogs bristle with horror.

In gratitude for these favours that little dog is expected to :

(*a*) Bark at tramps and suspicious characters, but not at the tradespeople or the postman.

(*b*) To be always clean and healthy and without fleas. (This is important.)

(*c*) To be always cheerful and pleased to see his owners, but not to show such pleasure by pawing their clothes.

(*d*) To allow himself to be ' played ' with by Baby, but not to snap or protest when tired or hurt.

4

An object to make the hackles of all
self-respecting dogs bristle with horror.

Placed in the far corner of the little yard
at the back

I'm sick of women.

(*e*) To eat with relish a daily menu of Spratt's dog biscuits, dry. (This is the most ' convenient ' food.)

(*f*) To be always at hand when required, but not press to come into the house, etc., etc.

There is one type of dog to be had, and one only, which conforms, if not to all these requirements, to most of them.

They can be bought now at varying prices from many of the
better-class ladies' outfitting establishments. They are
wonderfully made, no trouble to handle and they
never harbour fleas, or smell ; but perhaps
their most useful attribute of all is,
they are without heart, brains,
hopes or desires. So
convenient !

THE TWINS

MOODS OF "MAC"

THE INCORRUPTIBLE

Give a Dog a Bad Name

★   ★

GETTING the dog is a simple matter—naming him is another affair altogether. There is always a bit of risk attached to this christening business ; with the best intentions in the world it seems to be more or less of a gamble.

We have only to look around to see the truth of this. We all of us have friends and acquaintances whom we yearn to re-christen, those people who, it is perfectly obvious, have failed to grow up according to plan, and whose names, however proper and suitable at the christening, are somehow all wrong now. But this line of thought, interesting though it is, promises to become rather delicate ground if we pursue it very much further ; so back to the dogs !

The thing to remember then, when you've got your puppy, is not to be in too much of a hurry to christen him. First try to throw your mind forward to the time when the fascinating, wriggling armful has left puppy ways behind for ever, and has become a dog ; then go a little further still, and try and visualise your pup as a sober, staid old fellow at the ripe age of ten or twelve years. It seems an almost incredible state of affairs, but it is one that will, in the ordinary course of events, come about, provided you don't allow the pup to dig an early grave for himself with his teeth, or make too intimate an acquaintance with a motor car.

When you have taken this glimpse into the future it is safe to start thinking of a suitable name, not so easy a task as it promised to be at first though, because all those dear little names that you had previously thought of, and which would have been exactly right for the puppy, are no good now that you've looked ahead and realised that it's a dog for whom you want a name.

For large dogs one should beware of all those names that end in ' ie ', for there lie many pitfalls for the unwary. Some very attractive names for big sporting dogs, and certain of the terrier tribe, are to be found in the lists of hounds' names in hunting books ; a particularly

7

good selection, for instance, is in that immortal work, Peter Beckford's *Thoughts on Hunting*.

Sometimes one comes across a dog who has been christened in some happy moment, whose name is just right—when to think of one immediately brings the other to mind.

We once had, as children (I can only just remember him), a rather good, little, white Pomeranian, one of the old-fashioned type, when they bred them a trifle bigger than the midgets we see about to-day ; he was a winner at Cruft's and an uncommonly smart little sort. The most outstanding thing about that little dog (apart from his nine-inch coat which was a source of daily toil to one or other of us) was his carriage ; he walked with a tiny swagger, plumy tail carried just so, and his fringed legs he used almost like a hackney. His name was Walkly Sprite.

Another instance of a dog very happily named which occurs to me is a Sealyham terrier, which goes by the apparently ridiculous name of Bonnet ; but when you make Bonnet's acquaintance you know that the name is right ; she must always have been, is, and will remain just Bonnet to the end of the chapter. The poodle in the chair is Simoné, and rather happily named, I think, as she is feminine, fussy and French.

There are, and always will be, a large section of people who in this matter of names never stray off the safe and beaten tracks. That is why good old names like Roy, Spot, Rover or Prince will never die out, nor will Floss, Lassie, Nell or Gyp. But it is a pity that people when naming their pets do not give a little thought to the characteristics of the different breeds.

For example, I know a bull terrier, a particularly gingery specimen —the bite first and enquire afterwards sort—who has been burdened with the quite incongruous name of Prince ; not a bad sort of a name in its way perhaps but, tacked on to the dog in question, a glaring error of judgment. Fortunately Prince has risen above his name, and will doubtless continue to do so !

I came across a very amusing example of this lack of ' christening sense ' only the other day. I was walking along, when I heard a voice just behind me say :

8

I could have my chair if I could talk French!

WATCH ME!

' Come on, Lightning '.

The name attracted my attention at once ; I glanced round expecting to see, if not an Alsatian, then at least a lean and limber greyhound. But no ; pacing slowly along ten yards behind its owner was an ancient and incredibly fat and lethargic Airedale.

Unlike my bull terrier friend, this dog had evidently been unable
to rise above, or even keep level with, his name but had
just given up the unequal struggle in despair. But
what a miserable fate, to be steadily in-
creasing in girth, and yet to still be
answering to the name of
Lightning.

It Was a Famous Victory

★   ★

SHOW dogs are of many kinds ; some few would almost seem to have been born just to show, while others have with infinite labour, and an equally infinite capacity for taking pains, had a show career thrust upon them.

Quite a large number are show dogs from inclination, from sheer love of the game, and practise their hobby in and out of the ring, while others, and not a few, have not been born show dogs, cannot in any circumstances be made into show dogs, and consequently never will be show dogs.

'Rumpus', a Sealyham, belonged to the last category. In the beginning he and his Missus had both made up their minds, but unfortunately they had each made them up differently. The Missus made up her mind that she would like a show dog, and to that end she purchased a Sealyham, one Rumpus. But almost at once it was made plain to her that he definitely did not come into the first category, that, for whatever inscrutable purpose Rumpus had come into this world, it certainly was not to be a show dog.

But there remained the alternative of making him into one, and for many weary months, faithfully, daily, and without ceasing, did the Missus labour to that end. But she was up against heavy odds and the dice were loaded because, from his birth, Rumpus had been in the third category, and, also, because directly Rumpus discovered her intention he made up his mind that he wouldn't be a show dog, not in any circumstances, or under any conditions whatsoever. And so the battle began and went on and on.

In small things Rumpus won all along the line ; take for example that little matter of his whiskers. To be a successful show Sealyham it seems you must have what is known in the ' profession ' as ' furnishing ', your eyebrows, beard and whiskers must be profuse and it is essential that the latter should learn to grow, not as nature planned but straight downwards, to give the desired ' boxy ' square-jawed look.

10

Well, whiskers don't adapt themselves all in a day and so, to help them, the Missus once daily, and sometimes, when her enthusiasm was at its zenith, even twice a day, would brush the whiskers of Rumpus in a downward direction with a stiff hard brush.

And immediately after she had put the brush away (never before), Rumpus folded all his whiskers back again, until he looked as smug as Dickens's Mr. Chadband; but not content with this—he was a very thorough dog was Rumpus—he would deliberately and of set purpose wear those precious whiskers of his away; he scrubbed them off down holes and looking for mythical mice in the lumber room.

It was just the same with his 'coat'. Being, as we have said, in the third category, Rumpus hadn't been born with just the right texture of coat for a successful show Sealyham, therefore his Missus, who was nothing if not a 'tryer', had to do her best to make it into that. Most days she put powdered chalk on, which rose in clouds and made both Rumpus and his Missus nearly sneeze their heads off. Rumpus hated it, so immediately set about a counter move.

The moment he was released he made a quick bee-line for the wettest place he knew of and rolled in it, the muddier the better from the Sealyham's point of view.

Thus the battle went on until the great day dawned, the day on which the issue of the fight would be decided once and for all time—the day of the dog show. It was a memorable day for both Rumpus and the Missus.

They arrived at the show in good time, because the Missus wanted to put a last dose of chalk on Rumpus and attend to his whiskers. In the opinion of the Sealyham the whole show was an absolute 'frost'; to start with, all they received to eat were bits of dry biscuit, and then the prizes were not even bones or balls; all the dogs talked at once, and he couldn't get near enough to those he wanted to, for a good argument. But it was in the ring that Rumpus made his real serious stand against being a show dog.

He found it was after all fairly simple; all he had to do was to sit down, and keep on doing it. Every time the Missus placed him on his four serviceable stocky legs, they refused to support him, and he sank down in a floppy heap.

Everyone laughed except the Missus, who was scarlet in the face with mingled rage and mortification.

But it worked, oh most certainly it worked, because, as they left the ring, Rumpus, walking with cheery jauntiness, heard the Missus say, ' Never again, the little brute, never again '. She replaced him on the bench with a hearty thud, but Rumpus didn't mind that, he was a well-upholstered sort of dog. But all the same, he hadn't made his point quite clear yet—he proceeded to do so.

For the remainder of the day he crouched on his allotted bench the picture of misery ; he looked so dreadfully woebegone that everyone who passed stopped and said, ' Oh, what a pathetic-looking little chap, how miserable he looks ! Awful life a show dog's must be ! Poor little fellow ', and as they left they looked angrily and suspiciously at the Missus as though they suspected her of beating the ' poor little chap ' every time he didn't win a prize !

At five o'clock the Missus unfastened the chain, and Rumpus descended with joyous alacrity from the bench.

She led him off the show ground and all the way home in bitter silence. When they arrived, she opened her case and taking out the powdered chalk, she threw it on the fire. Rumpus watched her with pleased interest which increased noticeably when he saw her pick up the hated blue-and-white checked sheet which he had worn to keep his ' coat ' flat, and throw that into the fire too.

It was all quite satisfactory so far as it went, but he himself still felt far from comfortable, all dry and clean and tickly.

He went thoughtfully out into the garden and, down at the far end, he found what he had expected and hoped for—a large puddle where the rain had collected. He rolled himself in this, first one side and then the other, and, after that, to make a real job of it, he lay flat on his stomach in it.

Then, feeling much better, he trotted back to the house to show himself ; he found the Missus sitting with a book, and took up his position exactly in front of her, standing squarely on his large obstinate feet, while drops of dirty water trickled off him on to the carpet. She didn't look up.

' Hm,' thought Rumpus, ' sulky, eh ? ' He gave a short bark, and

12

RUMPUS AT THE SHOW

MISSED

as he still received no reply or acknowledgment of his presence, he shook himself violently. The answer he got then was the book which was called *Show Dogs, their Preparation.* Rumpus received it broadside on, but it left him unmoved, being a stolid heavy dog, besides which he still had one more point to make.

Watching the Missus with a wary eye, he carefully and
ostentatiously folded his whiskers as far back as he
could. After that he left the room quietly
and expeditiously, conscious of a
great   content—victory
was his.

THE EGOIST

"A hunting we will go!"

Little fat Badger and Tim
   have a day off

"Hi! You're in my bed."

His Proper Place

★ ★

THERE is a region one often hears alluded to as 'a dog's proper place'; but what, or where, we ask, is this mysterious spot? Is it at the end of a chain, or is it a little wooden box in a draughty out-house, or a yard behind iron bars? Can it be that it is in our own houses, in our armchairs and by our own fireside? The place varies as much as do the individuals who keep dogs. The end of a chain is the proper place for nothing, least of all for an intelligent, sensitive animal like a dog. Kept chained, only one part of a dog's nature develops, and that is the savage instinct. Even the chain running on a line is very little better; the dog can certainly get a little more freedom and movement, but, even so, it is a wretched existence. When we are considering the housing of the dog we can dismiss the chain method right away.

If the proper place is outside the house, then we must consider the little wooden box. The two essentials to bear in mind when a dog is to be housed out of doors are dryness and warmth. A dog will stand a lot of hard work and a certain amount of roughing it, but warm, dry sleeping quarters he must have. If these are damp and draughty, then, sooner or later, rheumatism, kennel lameness, or paralysis will, in all probability, be his portion.

There are a variety of good kennels on the market at the present time, some of which have open runs attached, others a covered yard; these runs not being intended to provide the inhabitant with his proper share of exercise, but merely so that he can enjoy a little fresh air and see a bit of what is going on in the fascinating outside world.

If a dog is to be kept clean he will require a bed of fresh straw every two days. Wheat straw makes the best bed; the other kind is too brittle. But all kinds of straw, unless changed frequently, tend to harbour fleas and dirt and are bad for the dog's skin. Hay of any kind as bedding is an abomination. The kennel and yard should be brushed out daily, and at least twice a year limewashed.

And now for those kindly individuals who are of the opinion that a

15

dog's proper place is with us in our houses. A dog will sleep better and more quietly if he has a definite place appointed to him. Dogs have a very strong sense of possession, and, even though the sleeping place be only a rug put down in some corner, once the dog has realised it is his, he will prefer it to a silken eiderdown in any other part of the house. There are at the present time a large number of dog baskets for sale; the majority of these are more ornamental than useful. They are apt to be draughty and many of them have floors that radiate to a peak in the centre. This pattern is, of course, quite useless. Some of the more expensive of these dog beds are lined and quilted. These look very attractive, and with the dog inside make a pretty picture. But the picture has a reverse side; the lining of the basket, in a week or two, becomes soiled, and, probably, the padding gets loosened, and the bed develops curious lumps and humps. If the dog could speak he would very likely tell us that the bed was now only fit for the cat to occupy, and he would be quite right. If a basket is insisted upon, a piece of old blanket, folded and big enough to fit the basket, is preferable.

The basket should occupy a place free from draughts, but should not be put close to the fireside. Another sleeping place for the indoor dog is a rug or blanket put in an armchair. This is a good, practical method of solving the indoor housing problem, and one which is, as a rule, very popular with dogs. It is high off the ground, and in consequence free from draughts, and, altogether, makes a very snug bed.

And now we come to that select brigade who are so misguided as to wish to enjoy the company of their small friends by night as well as by day. Their argument is that, twelve short years being the normal span of a dog's life, it is the height of folly that half of that brief period should be spent shut away from his owners. This is the contention of the downright dog-lover in the most literal sense of that much-abused term. Provided the dog sleeps on, and not in, his owner's bed, this choice of sleeping place is quite harmless—that is, to the dog. Whether that also applies to the quilt is another story ! Some people argue that this method of sleeping a dog softens him, and spoils a terrier for sport. This is not the case, as a well-known sporting terrier enthusiast slept with no fewer than six of his pets on his bed, and many a good day's

16

A CUCKOO IN THE NEST

EYE

sport they showed with otter, stoat and rat.   Sharing his owner's bed never yet spoilt any terrier worthy of the name.   What saps the sporting spirit of these little fellows is keeping them from their legitimate jobs, and never letting them ' have a go ' at ratting, fighting, or any of those pursuits which are the very salt of life to them.

To sum up this housing question, you will be accommodating
your dog excellently if you do unto him as you would
do to yourself.   You will then have the
pleasurable knowledge that half of
that short life is spent
in comfort.

The Bruiser

★   ★

I KNEW the Bruiser (that isn't his real name, of course) by sight for a long time before I made his acquaintance. Most days he would be out in the town threading his way through the crowded streets with easy assurance, and after I got to know him he always gave me a friendly wag of his elegant whip tail as he passed. He was generally by himself, and I came to look out for the handsome liver-and-white bull terrier with the knowing bloodshot eyes.

There are certain dogs that I always wish had the gift of speech—the Bruiser is one of them. If he could talk, the first thing that I should ask him to tell me would be why, on one memorable night, he ran away from a small terrier.

The Bruiser is the premier fighting dog of the town, and his victories are legion. Every dog who passes in the street he challenges, but his sinister fame is too well known; very few dogs care to take up the Bruiser's challenge, which is just why his rout by a little terrier is so inexplicable.

It happened like this.

The Bruiser when on duty is the guardian of a small hotel, and a very efficient watchman he makes. I was sitting in the bar one evening, having a drink before dinner; at the next table were two people and on the knees of one of them sat a small tan-and-grizzled terrier with the most intelligent eyes, and the sharpest expression I have ever seen on the face of terrier before or since. It sat bolt upright like a canine interrogation mark, scanning each person as they came in, and every now and again a growl would rumble in its little throat. I caught myself wondering idly what would happen if the watchman of the hotel, the Bruiser, appeared.

Hardly had the thought passed through my brain when the swing doors began to revolve and in three seconds the familiar liver-and-white form appeared and strolled into the bar with 'owner' written large on his tight-lipped inscrutable countenance.

The sight of him seemed to electrify that little terrier; with a snarl of hatred he sprang off his owner's knees, and launched his fifteen pounds of grizzled hair and meagre bone against the fifty-six pounds of whipcord-like sinew, bone and muscle that was the Bruiser. For a breathless moment there was complete silence, then the incredible happened.

Before the terrier could close, the Bruiser had turned and was out of the bar like a streak ; the last I saw of him was his elegant white whip tail disappearing round the door marked 'Private'. As the miracle happened the barmaid dropped a glass and said breathlessly :

'Well, I don't know ! That's the first time I've ever seen our dog turn his tail ! '

The owner of the little terrier in the excitement of the moment had knocked over a glass of beer, but had managed to pick up that snarling ' wick ' little morsel of grizzled hair and knife-like spirit that had routed the famous Bruiser in his own bar.

I went thoughtfully out pondering on the miracle that
had just taken place, and that is why I wish
that my friend the Bruiser had
the gift of speech.

THE BRUISER.

An impression.

TIRED

TINKER AND HIS PALS

BLINKERS GOES WALKING

When NOT Behind

He's in FRONT.

Dogs on Leads

★   ★

EXERCISE, besides being essential to a dog's health, is, or should be, one of the main pleasures of his life. A dog that is not regularly exercised very soon finds the time hang heavily, and, taking it upon himself to remedy this distressing state of affairs, as a rule gets into mischief. He loses himself, becomes a town 'ranger', or an indiscriminate chaser of everything that moves, be it upon legs or wheels, and often finishes his career under a motor car. All dogs should have a couple of walks a day, and if one of these is in the town on a lead the other should be, if possible, a free run. If the dog is 'traffic wise' and is out with his owner the lead can be dispensed with, but if out with a servant, or some other member of the household who will not keep that watchful eye peculiar as a rule to owners only, then the dog is safer on a leash.

It is the free run with his owner that is the delight of the dog, and, even should the time given up to this entail a little self-sacrifice, it should be remembered that a dog's entire life is really a sacrifice to the whims and pleasures of his owner. Contrary to some ideas, it is not the person who feeds him who holds the magic key to a dog's heart ; it is the one who provides and shares his pleasures. And there is no doubt that a country walk with the 'boss' or the 'missus' constitutes one of the dog's greatest joys. Of course, when I say a country walk that is just what I mean—a real, genuine country walk with plenty of mud, rabbits, and smells about, and perhaps, if we are really whole-hearted, a bit of nice bog and a stream or two to ford, one of those streams for preference whose crumbling banks are the homes of water-rats. It is a sorry sight to see a dog walking in the country at the end of a taut leash. From every tuft of grass which holds some mysterious and entrancing smell, from every hole and every line of scent, he is dragged remorselessly away and hurried along on what must be to him a meaningless promenade.

A great deal of the intense pleasure experienced by a dog during a country walk is conveyed to him through his nose. The world of a dog is teeming with elusive smells, all of which are of interest and worthy of investigation. To drag a dog along on a lead in the country is somewhat similar to hurrying a child through a huge toy-shop and never letting him stop to look or touch. Besides, just watch an active dog stretching his limbs and galloping over the grass for the sheer joy of movement, glorying in the ecstasy of his own speed ; then think of the misery of the same dog always checked, always trammelled by the hated lead.

To some of the big active breeds galloping is an essential if they are to be kept in anything like trim. The Alsatian, Great Dane, or Irish wolfhound will easily do ten miles a day beside a horse and be all the better for it. Galloping on the roads behind a bicycle is not good for a dog ; a certain amount of road exercise is necessary to harden the feet, but it should be slow. Of course the type and length of exercise varies with the different breeds. A bulldog does not require as much exercise as a terrier, and a Pekingese or Japanese spaniel will not thank you for a long walk over heather, but at the same time walks they must have. A dog turned into the garden for the purpose of exercising himself does nothing of the kind. He, figuratively speaking, mooches about with his hands in his pockets and is profoundly and devastatingly bored. If two or three dogs are kept and turned on to the lawn then they will play with each other if they are fairly young dogs, but this form of exercise is not so good as a walk.

Deprived of proper exercise dogs grow fat and lethargic, and a fat dog, besides being an offence against nature, is a nuisance to himself and is rarely healthy. It is not always convenient to turn out again to take the dog for his walk, but, once out, and seeing the pleasure the dog is getting from it, soon puts heart into his owner.

Roy the Ranger

★　　★

JUST as there are 'men about town', so there are dogs. Cool, collected sorts, these dogs who when you meet them, should you happen to be an acquaintance of theirs, give you just a passing glance and a careless, jaunty wag of the tail.

Roy the Ranger is one of these. He is a tricolour collie, a bit on the small side, but more than making up in assurance that which he lacks in inches. He is to be seen in all places at all times, always alone, trotting along in a cheeky, independent manner, his banner of a tail carried at a cocksure 'you be blowed' angle. Most dogs he passes with a scornful, slightly pitying air, and if they have the misfortune to be on leads his contempt is positively withering.

On very rare occasions he may be seen accompanying his owner, but one gets the impression when he does so that it is merely a gracious concession on Roy's part, a kindly act just to show there is a slight connection between the two of them.

Roy the Ranger is one of those who will always prefer to plough a lone furrow, and on one never-to-be-forgotten night he very nearly succeeded in ploughing himself into a better world.

He was making his usual casual way home, stopping for a word here and a snarl or an exchange of compliments there, when, just as he stepped off the pavement and started to saunter across the road, there was a blinding glare of light and a shriek of outraged brakes. Roy had disappeared under the bonnet of a large motor car, which had swung round the corner just a bit faster than it should have done.

Roy the Ranger is well known in his own neighbourhood and in a very few minutes a little crowd had gathered round what appeared to be the lifeless form of the Ranger, who lay in a huddled, limp heap, his gallant banner of a tail draggled in the mud, a scarlet stream trickling steadily from a deep cut across his flank.

The driver of the car stood miserably by, and hoped audibly that the brute wasn't dead, and privately was quite sure that he was. The crowd pressed closer and stood round, in the customary futile way of

23

human beings in the mass, loudly voicing their comments, advice and opinions and obviously hugely enjoying the accident.

There was a growing chorus of ' poor old chap ', ' oh, the poor dog ', ' reckon he's dead ', and ' leastways if he aint now he soon will be ', and ' these 'ere road 'ogs ! ' at which the face of the unfortunate driver of the offending car took unto itself a distinctly redder tinge.

But all this didn't help Roy the Ranger, who still lay motionless and bleeding, but suddenly there was a stir in the crowd and the provider of the Ranger's food and licence elbowed his way through the throng. He knelt down beside the limp form, and then he stood up with the Ranger in his arms, the blood still trickling down, and directed the cause of the accident to open the door of his car and drive him and the victim to the nearest veterinary surgeon's. The young man, though he gazed a little ruefully at the blood, was quite willing, even anxious to do what he could.

The owner of the Ranger got in, the collie in his arms, the young man sprang in and started up his engine, and the car moved away, leaving a slightly disappointed crowd feeling rather flat now that the main cause of their enjoyment and interest—the victim—had been removed.

The vet. washed and cleaned the deep gash—which had only very narrowly missed a big artery—put a few stitches in, and in twenty minutes Roy the Ranger went home by car, looking a trifle under the weather and not quite his jaunty self.

If this were a story with a moral to it the conclusion would be that, after his accident, Roy the Ranger turned over a new leaf, ceased to roam, and was miraculously transformed into a sober ' stay at home and mind the baby ' sort of dog.

But this being a true story about a real dog we must be truthful. So then, ten days after his accident saw Roy the Ranger making his jaunty way through the streets, plumy tail carried high, and his bold roving glance always on the look-out for friend or foe, equally ready to have a neighbourly ' crack ' or to pick a quarrel.

Just the same old Roy the Ranger—but with a
deeply rooted prejudice against
all motor traffic.

24

Still the same old Roy the Ranger

We've got a rabbit
   but I did most of it.

"JERRY.
In memory.

The Dog's Menu

★   ★

THERE are almost endless theories relating to the feeding of dogs, good, bad and indifferent; the best thing to do is to apply a little common sense, and once again put yourself in the other fellow's place. Remember, if your dog is to enjoy his meals and derive any benefit from them, he must be fed at regular hours out of clean dishes, and there should be a certain amount of variety in the food. The dog biscuit manufacturers, it is true, have solved a good many difficulties for us, but a diet of nothing but dog biscuits gets monotonous and is not good for the dog.

Two meals a day are sufficient for the adult dog in health. The main meal at midday and a few biscuits in the evening, about six o'clock, make a fairly practical time-table. If the dog is given his main meal then, he has a chance to exercise afterwards, and this method tends to keep the kennel cleaner, and is more comfortable also for the dog who sleeps indoors.

There are plenty of ways in which the canine menu can be varied. For the solid part of the midday meal, boiled rice, stale bread (brown or white), suet pudding and plain dog biscuit are all good. These should have boiling soup poured over, and meat cut up and added. A sheep's head makes a nice change and splendid broth; boiled liver is also much appreciated. If a large number of dogs are kept, horse beef can generally be got fairly cheaply from the local knacker. A good change of food in spring and summer, and one which most dogs appreciate, is fish; the jaw-pieces and trimmings of cod and hake, when well boiled in milk and water and then mixed with dry dog biscuits broken up small, make a very appetising meal. The evening feed of dry biscuits can be varied, but they should for preference be of a plain variety. In passing, tame rabbits and chickens, though excellent eating, should not appear in the menu!

Should a dog refuse his food for any reason, do not try to tempt him; remove the bowl at once and do not offer him anything until his next meal time comes round, but do not give him the same food again then. Stale food is particularly obnoxious to dogs. A good food for a dog who is ill, or off his feed, is stewed rabbit ; dogs are inordinately fond of this, and will very often take it when everything else is refused.

Bones of the right kind are good for dogs, but merely as dessert— no game, fish, rabbit or mutton bones should be given, they splinter and chip too easily. Big beef bones are the best, and these should be given to the dog after he has had his ordinary meal ; he will then only gnaw bits off his bone and play with it.

In the spring and summer a little flowers of sulphur mixed with his food keeps a dog's coat in condition and acts as a blood cooler. Some people advocate green vegetables boiled and mixed with the meat and biscuit ; if the dogs will eat them, this is a very good blood purifier, but unfortunately dogs, being by nature eaters of flesh, often will not touch the green stuff.

The things to avoid in feeding dogs are sweets, cakes and all kinds of odd ' bits '. It is a delightful thought that our dog shares all our joys and sorrows, but when it comes to sharing with him our breakfasts, lunches, teas and dinners, it is time to pull ourselves up with a stern hand, and turn a deaf ear to those heartbreaking whines, and a yet blinder eye to those tragic ones fixed upon us so beseechingly that they, if ours are not very blind indeed, will certainly win in the end. For, remember, the power of the human eye is as nothing to the power of the dog's ! Denied the gift of tongues, he has been given instead extraordinarily eloquent eyes, and, while we can quite successfully resist the eyes of our friend's dogs, alas ! when we come to our own—well of course we know exactly what the little chap is trying so hard to tell us— and all is lost, we succumb at once. And at no time are the dog's eyes so piteous and heart-rending as when he is bending all his energies in an effort to obtain those delicious and illicit bits that his heart craves.

Now, then is the time to harden your heart, spare the food,
and save your dog from—an ugly figure, false teeth
and an early grave ; three disasters which, though
we cannot always avoid them for ourselves, we can at least do our best to
prevent from overtaking
our dogs !

26

CONFABULATION—

JUBILATION!

DAVID AND JONATHAN

David and Jonathan

★   ★

AT one time I used to see them quite a lot, first the big, shaggy, solemn bobtail, with a coat in colour something between a pea-soup fog and the smoke from a wood fire when the fuelling is green and wet, a magnificent, though rather dirty, white ruff, and fierce, light eyes, true Border sheep-dog eyes, which peered out from under a perfect cascade of hair.

Always about half a dozen yards behind him, pattering importantly along on his rather inadequate legs, was one of the royal dogs of China ; it had a pale golden-yellow coat, sweeping ear fringes, large, pathetic goggle eyes, and a wide, frog-like mouth.

If the bobtail thought he was getting too far in front of his small friend he stopped and patiently waited until the small, puffing, yellow midget had drawn level again.

I never knew their names, or who owned them, but to myself I always called them David and Jonathan ; David was the benign, tolerant, calm bobtail, and Jonathan the fussy, important Pekingese.

David always minded his own business, he never stopped to speak to other dogs but just plodded heavily on his way, his only thought, apart from getting on with the job in hand, seemed to be Jonathan, who took a bit of looking after; he would stop to sniff and investigate this, and that. I used to feel sorry for David, he appeared to do such a lot of waiting about while Jonathan fussed and pottered with trifles.

They came out in all weathers, and no matter was it wet and cold, or warm and sunny, the weather never seemed to be quite right for them somehow.

If it were raining, then David's enormous woolly coat became a dank, wet mass, and as for Jonathan—well, Jonathan merely looked like two-penn'orth of draggled, yellow, wispy hair trailing miserably through the mud.

I often wondered why Jonathan came out in bad weather ; he obviously detested walking in the rain. But even on a wet day Jonathan couldn't walk briskly ; it was pathetic to see David standing on the street corner, waiting to see Jonathan safely across the road, the rain pouring down on to his dripping shaggy coat, and Jonathan some way behind sniffing futilely at probably nothing at all, his ridiculous leg fringes sweeping the mud, while he looked as cross and scowling as the weather.

But on warm days they seemed if anything more uncomfortable, because David was still wearing his winter woollies, and his long pink ribbon of tongue would be always lolling out ; and little Jonathan wasn't in much better case, his large frog-like mouth would be gaping wide, and he would toil along in the heat behind David, on his little bowed legs, his breath coming in snorts and pants through his small squashed nose. Strange companions David and Jonathan, but it is said that sometimes opposites make the best friends.

It seemed true enough in this case, because though I met them together on scores of occasions, I never saw David without Jonathan, or Jonathan without David.

'Excuse me but I'm afraid
I must be going now!'

I chose
the largest bed

"Me, Paddy."

Where are those ratsandrabbits!

Paddy

PORTRAIT OF A LADY

★   ★

I AM wire-haired, black, tan and white, and though you might not guess it from my name I am a lady, but not just an ordinary sort of lady ; I know this because they have a paper in the house explaining the special kind of lady I am. I always hoped they would have the paper framed and hung up where people could see it ; but no, it was just hidden away in a drawer, as we hide our bones, and what I am afraid of is that when they want to dig it up they will forget where it is buried. People are so dreadfully careless, I find.

To-day has been a very important occasion—my birthday. I don't know whether it was a specially good sort of birthday, because I can't remember my first one, and this was only my second.

It began really yesterday evening when they had me all retrimmed and washed and messed about ; still, to give them their due, I must say I did look rather nice when it was finished ; I certainly do ' pay for dressing ', as the saying is.

My birthday itself started quite well, by my Missus taking me on a 'bus. I like going on 'buses and I believe she does too. When we got out of the 'bus we walked about looking at things.

I met quite a lot of dogs and ladies I should have liked to become better acquainted with, but each time we started getting to know each other my Missus pulled the leash, and I had to say, ' Excuse me, but I am afraid I must be going now '. So annoying ! But really, what with motor cars, errand boys and ' prams ', not to mention people with huge clumsy feet and hard heels, it's hardly safe for a lady to be out in the town without a leash, nuisances though they are.

After a time we met a Person and we all went into a big room, and had bits to eat and drink, at least they had both but I had only bis-cuits ; they forgot to order me anything to drink—human beings I find are so careless. That is in my opinion their worst fault. But every time they became very much engrossed in their own bits and forgot to

29

pass the biscuits, I just stood up and planted both paws on the table-cloth. That made them remember at once what they'd forgotten—me.

After they'd finished their bits the Person said something about a present, it being my birthday; that sounded all right so long as the present was of the right kind.

We went off to find a shop to buy my present; and I can tell you I looked very anxiously at each shop we passed. I thought and hoped that they were looking for a butcher's shop—but no, they weren't. Then I thought they might be going to buy me a rabbit—that would have been something like a present, eh? But, after all the fuss, what do you think the present turned out to be? A leash!

Well, I felt this was a pretty poor sort of a birthday, and after that I wasn't even surprised when my Missus handed me over to the Person, and left me, waved her hand and left me, just like that. However, I always make the best of things, and the Person let me play and bite the lead all the way—I think she thought that if she didn't I might stop and sit down and refuse to go. I might have, too, after that birthday gift! I might have done anything! After a short walk we came to a house and went in, up some stairs and into a room—it was a funny room, full of all sorts of things, books, papers, clothes, whips and a bridle, and boots, and some foxes' and hares' heads, dead ones, stuck on little bits of board, very silly they looked to me.

The Person said she'd be ' back in a minute ', and left me standing there; never asked me to sit down or anything.

I saw there were two beds in the room, one a sort of round small one made out of a basket, and the other a much larger one with an eider-down on. Well, the small one looked rather messy, as though the Person had just jumped out in a hurry and left it unmade, so I chose the larger bed and curled up there, and was just dropping off when back came the Person. I wasn't too pleased to see her until I noticed that she was carrying a plate with pieces of meat on it, then I woke up a bit.

When I saw her get a piece of paper out and a pencil and stare at me, I knew what the game was; it was my likeness that she was after!

There was once a famous picture called ' Portrait of a Lady '. I expect she was going to do one just like it and that's why she had chosen me to what they call ' sit ' for it.

30

I soon found out how to play the game. When she spoke to me I just gave her a quick passing glance and then looked away, so that she had to pick up a piece of meat. Well, of course, I took a good look at that you may be sure, for one thing to make certain that the Person didn't eat it herself.

While she was doing my portrait I kept hearing howls and wails. I was rather worried at first and wondered what sort of place I had come to—and this in spite of the beef, which was of quite good quality —until I heard a furious scratching at the door, the handle rattled, and a very cross voice snarled :

' I know you've got a dog in there ! Who is it ? You needn't try and hide it, and if you let it go in my bed, or in our bed either, I shall fight it directly I get in. Open the door at once.'

The Person said :

' You be quiet and mind your own business, and go and lie down.'

I said nothing ; the voice sounded rather common ; besides I'm not a dog, I'm a lady, so there was no occasion for me to say anything.

I quite enjoyed myself until the meat was finished ; after that it became a little tiresome, if you understand me. So when the Person suddenly said, ' I'm tired of this, shall we go and look for " ratsan'- rabbits " ? ' I agreed at once.

So we set off, and were joined by a black-and-tan dog who rushed up in an awful ' to do ', and asked me all sorts of things : who I was ? if I had had anything to eat ? if I'd been in his bed ?—all kinds of idiotic things. I said I really hadn't time to answer all his questions as we were going to look for ' ratsan'rabbits '.

' Huh ! ' he said, ' a fat lot of " ratsan'rabbits " you'll find, I don't think. You're too dressy by half ! '

Then he tore on in front. Poor manners I thought he had.

But he was right about one thing, because, although we went into some fields and woods, and I looked carefully in every tree root, and in all the gorse bushes, I couldn't find any ratsandrabbits at all.

It was night when I reached home ; rather a trying day, but birthdays only come once a year, and I hope next year that my present won't be a leash.

31

Spots

★ ★

I WAS musing idly on the subject of proverbs the other day : ' Can the leopard change his spots ?   Ridiculous ! '

I spoke aloud without thinking, when—

' No, of course, he can't, but a bull terrier can all the same.'

I started and looked down ; the voice belonged to the White Hope who lay in a patch of sunlight, a grin on his subtle, wedge-shaped face and his little, pink-rimmed eyes twinkling as he noted my astonishment.

I watched him mesmerising a large fly that had settled on his flank. Snap ! The pink and white jaws clashed, and the fly disappeared.

' Quick work ', remarked the White Hope complacently.   ' Beats your fly-papers, eh ?   Eh ? ' he said again sharply, lifting one side of his tightly-folded lips enquiringly.

' Oh rather ! Yes ! ' I replied hastily.   ' But you were saying something about a bull terrier being able to change his spots, weren't you ? '

' Well, I might have ', he said lazily, sucking one of his pink pads that always looked, to me, unpleasantly naked.

' But ', I persisted, ' that's impossible.   A bull terrier couldn't change his spots because he hasn't got any.'

' I had some once ', remarked the White Hope blandly.

' Rats ! ' I retorted.

' Spots, I said.'

The White Hope sniggered rudely, and rolled over luxuriously to let the sun warm his sleek pink and white stomach, while I sat and watched him, thinking how very like a pig he looked.

In a few minutes he rolled back again, and glanced up, his little dark eyes glinting slyly.

' About those spots of mine ', he said loudly, and then stopped, evidently waiting for me to say something, but I didn't.   He looked, I fancied, just a trifle disappointed as he went on with the tale : ' You remember that Dismal Desmond the Boss got ?   " Plum puddings " they call 'em ? '

I nodded.

32

THE WHITE HOPE

who goes?

More impressions
of the White Hope.

The FLY.

'Well, the Boss bought him, if you remember, to run under the dog-cart; thought one of the spotted sort made a better-looking turn-out, matched the piebald cob and that, and looked smarter than an all-white dog, though to my thinking self colours are better taste every time, eh?'

The White Hope paused here and eyed me intently:

'*Eh?*' I said. He lifted his mottled lips, exposing one white and shining canine.

'Well, of course', I said quickly, 'goes without saying, surely?'

'Well, say it. Better manners', muttered the White Hope, folding his lips down neatly.

I waited in silence for quite three minutes while he pretended to be busy cleaning his paws and biting the end of his whip tail.

'Where was I?' he said at last, rather ungraciously. 'Oh, yes; well, the Boss was never happy until he'd got one of these idiotic plum pudding Dismal Desmonds; he called it Buck, why do you think?'

I shook my head dutifully.

'Why, short for Buchanan, the Black and White Whisky bloke; name suited his spots all right, but nothing else; if ever a dog was short of " buck " and spirit that dog was Buck.'

It sounded a bit incoherent, but I knew what he meant all right.

'Ah', I said, 'a pity that.'

'Yes,' went on the White Hope, ' if a dog so much as looked at him, it gave him the jim-jams, and of course, in time, the dogs round about, the lads of the village as it were, got to know and to watch out for friend Buck. There was one in particular, a big cross-bred Airedale and collie, lives at the Bay Horse; well, he made it his main job in life to put fear into Buck; every time he went out with the dog-cart this beggar from the " pub " would be lying in wait to roll old spots in the mud.'

'Too bad!' I murmured.

The White Hope grinned and proceeded.

'At last the Boss got so that he couldn't stand it any longer. " We'll have to get rid of Buck, my dear ", he said to the Missus one day. " Why not take Stingo with you once, to frighten the dog off? " she suggested, meaning me. Stingo is my ordinary name, you know. " No good ", said the Boss, " the beggar knows old Stingo a mile off,

33

and wouldn't come out." He had cause to, too ', said the White Hope, again lifting his lip. ' Then the Boss had his great idea. " I've got it ", he shouted, banging his fist on the table. I forgot to mention they were feeding at the time. " We'll disguise Stingo." " How—what on earth do you mean ? " asked the Missus, who, between ourselves, isn't too quick on to the bone, if you take my meaning. " We'll give him some spots ", said the Boss, chuckling. Well, they did ; that very day they took me into the saddle-room and painted dozens and dozens of black spots all over me. I felt no end of a guy, and there sat that miserable brute of a Buck smiling all over his silly-looking mug. Of course he smiled ; I was going out to be the lamb to draw the tiger, so to speak.'

I made a slight sound, and the White Hope looked up suspiciously.

' Lamb, I said ', he repeated firmly, and resumed his story. ' In a few hours the spots were dry, and, as the Boss was as anxious as a kid to try the experiment, he ordered the dog-cart and off we went. It was a joke, the Boss was grinning, and so was the Missus. I was smiling a bit too as I entered into the spirit of the thing and trotted under the cart in proper Dismal Desmond style ; even the piebald cob was chortling. As we drew near the " pub ", I peered anxiously out between the cob's legs ; it would be a bit of a sell if, after all our trouble, the brute wasn't there. But it was all right. He was waiting, as usual, and no sooner did he catch a glimpse of my black and white spots than he launched himself at me and was in the air when he realised that they were only borrowed ones ! My eye, I did give him a trouncing and a half ! I should have killed him if the Boss hadn't dragged me off—it was prime ! ' Here the White Hope shut his eyes and grinned.

' What became of Buck ? ' I ventured to enquire.

The little red-rimmed eyes blinked, and the White Hope yawned.

' Oh, him ? A Pekingese spoke to him, and the poor feller was so upset he ran under the wheel of his own dog-cart ; no loss either ', said the White Hope callously.

He coiled himself up tightly, and folded his white whip tail neatly round his nose. After a minute he opened one eye :

' That's the end of the story ', he said smoothly.

I took the hint and went.

34

"Lu wind 'im lads, Lu wind 'im!"

Kendall and District Otter Hounds

"Please I've come!"

The Uninvited Guest

★ ★

IT was nearly time for lunch, when a series of short shrill barks sounded at the front door. 'Visitors', I thought, and then, 'what a stupid inconvenient time to come!'

I heard the maid go to the door, and had just succeeded in schooling my face into slightly more welcoming lines, when I heard the front door close again, and then a quick pattering gallop on the stairs, and a small body hurled itself against the door of my room, which, as usual, was insecurely fastened.

It burst open now, and in tumbled an excited, bustling, white form, evidently in a great hurry; her small, dark eyes twinkled with delight, and a rose-pink tongue gave me energetic greeting.

It was Peggy, my sometime model, evidently come to pay a friendly call; I laughed in my relief, visitors of this kind being always welcome.

Meanwhile Peggy, or Pegtops as I always call her, was sitting on the rug gazing up at me with an enquiring air. She didn't look quite like settling down, and yet it was perfectly clear that she had no intention of taking her departure.

She continued to sit 'doggedly'—and this just describes her attitude—upon the hearth-rug.

I made a few polite remarks, to which she replied with a vigorous short white tail, but it became more and more evident as time went on that something was lacking.

Peggy is too well bred to look openly bored, but I could see that things were not quite coming up to her expectations. I racked my brains wondering where the snag could be, and expending, I have no doubt, far more thought upon my small wire-haired guest, than I should have done over one of her human sisters. I was still pondering over the problem when the luncheon gong sounded.

Up sprang Pegtops, tail wagging gaily, and her small, black eyes snapping with excitement.

'Come on, let's go and see about that food', she seemed to be saying.

'Of course, the explanation was simple ', I thought, as we
went together to the dining-room, my small guest now
perfectly cheerful and happy, and registering
pleased anticipation from cocked ears to
quivering stern.   'Pegtops had
come to lunch.'

THE UNKNOWN QUANTITY

"Magpie" of the Three Harrows

Time, Gentlemen!

★　　　★

MAGPIE of the Three Harrows arranged his large, piebald self more comfortably, yawned cavernously, exposing gleaming, white fangs, closed his deep-set, golden eyes, and sighed heavily.

It had been a rather trying day and as usual all the trouble that had arisen was due to his being an outsize in dogs. Measuring thirty-six inches at the shoulder, he weighed a hundred and thirty pounds and was as big as a fair-sized calf. His large size, coupled with his drip white coat, spotted and mottled with irregular splashes of glossy black, made him an outstanding dog in any company.

Other and lesser dogs loathed him, the mere sight in the distance of the majestic form of the big Harlequin was enough to send them into snarling, yapping hysterics. In twos and threes, they would trot along behind him, like bad-mannered little street urchins, yelping and snapping at his heels. If they went too far, Magpie would turn round and seize one of them in his great jaws and give him a shake ; the worst of it was that sometimes he forgot the power in those jaws of his and crushed the life out of the offender altogether if it happened to be a small dog.

Magpie opened his yellow eyes and stretched his great forelegs that were as straight and hard as gun-barrels. He was a rather lazy dog, but then his life was such an idle one ; his ' Missus ' was the genial if rather sharp-tongued landlady of the Three Harrows, and the sole job of work which Magpie performed in return for his keep was, every night at 10.30, to go into the tap-room and bark, ' Time, Gentlemen ! ' in his deep booming voice.

Strangers to the Three Harrows viewed the huge, piebald form askance and, generally, made a hasty unostentatious departure, but the regular patrons regarded Magpie as rather a joke, though none of them stayed to argue with him.

As he lay in his accustomed place in the shelter of an old oak dresser, from which he could view all who went into the tap-room, Magpie grunted sleepily ; it had been a strenuous day.

To begin with there had arrived by the morning's post one of those

37

petitions sometimes called ' Round Robins ', to the effect that a certain number of people in the immediate neighbourhood required the execution or extradition—the former for preference—of one, Magpie, of the Three Harrows. These petitions were nothing new, the huge dog had enemies all round the district, but still it was hardly a cheery start for the day.

After the petition had found its way into the fire, Magpie had gone out for a short stroll. ' And mind you keep outer mischief, yer great daft gomeril ! ' his Missus had shouted after him in good-natured warning. Magpie, his mind as void of evil as that of a new-born puppy, stalked majestically up the road, his intentions, like many another's, pure and good ; but—well, little things will happen. He was strolling slowly along, when he beheld coming towards him, growling and snuffling, a small dog of China. And if there was one sort of dog more than any other that, so to speak, got Magpie's ' goat ', it was one of China's national breed.

He stepped off the sidewalk, eyeing the small, lion-like creature on its absurd bowed legs, with uneasy dislike. But, instead of passing quietly by on the other side, the Pekingese seemed determined to get into trouble ; perhaps he was tired of life, or possibly he was merely feeling a bit liverish, and instead of a small dog, a thoughtless and unkind Providence had set this lurid-looking, spotted monster in his path. At all events the dog of China waddled right on to his fate, growling and snorting, his large eyes goggling furiously.

Seen at close quarters, the incredibly flat face and rolling, prominent eyes completely upset the big Harlequin. Scowling, he dropped his heavy head, and made a chop at that brave, but foolhardy, little dog of China, who, in less than a minute, was dangling limply from the massive jaws of Magpie, who resumed his stroll, carrying his strange parcel in a casual, offhand manner.

A little further on he saw an acquaintance of his, and deciding that he had taught the Pekingese a sufficiently sharp lesson, and feeling rather tired of the burden, he dropped it carelessly down. But what was this ? Instead of getting up all the better for his lesson in good manners, the dog of China lay still on the pavement, his goggle eyes staring fixedly at nothing. Magpie eyed him for a moment in surprise and then sniffed at him, as if suspicious that the little dog was 'shamming'. 'Some mistake here?' but it never moved at all.

However, carelessly dismissing the matter from his mind, Magpie of the Three Harrows resumed his stroll. And that was the morning.

In the afternoon as he lay on the warm flags in the sun in front of the inn, a circus went by, a long procession of caravans and chestnut, white and piebald horses and ponies. He watched them pass with lazy indifference, his yellow eyes half shut; but if his interest in the circus was only slight, that of the circus, or rather its proprietor, in him was just the reverse.

The proprietor descended from his caravan, and walking across to the Three Harrows, he regarded the enormous, recumbent, spotted form of Magpie with a shrewd appraising gaze.

'Just the very ticket', he murmured, gloating over the showy appearance and generous proportions of the big, drowsy hound, and he went round to the back door of the Three Harrows—it being out of hours he couldn't go in from the bar entrance.

Magpie continued to lie basking in the pleasant warmth for a few minutes, then, as the man failed to come out again, the big dog lumbered to his feet and strolled round to the back door.

No sign of the stranger, but Magpie's big blunt nose told him that he was still on the premises. He pushed at the half-shut kitchen door and, standing for a moment framed in the doorway, he saw a strange sight. The landlady, Magpie's Missus, was standing, hands planted firmly on her hips, watching the circus proprietor who was engaged in covering the kitchen table with a novel kind of cloth consisting of Treasury notes. Neither of them saw the black and white dog for a minute, and the showman went on counting out the notes.

'Fifty-five, fifty-eight, sixty!' he said triumphantly. 'You can buy a dozen dogs with them, Missus. I've been looking for just such a dog as that of your'n for months. I want him to put in the bill, a pony act, " smallest pony in the world, eight hands high, walks under dog". A real draw it were, an' then blest if my old dog, " Tiger ", didn't go and die on me.'

Here the showman gave a start as some of the bank-notes fluttered; Magpie had come up and, resting his enormous piebald head on the

39

table, was sniffing contemptuously at the bits of crackling paper. His Missus looked at him proudly and then turned to the stranger :

' Nay, I'm none selling ', she said firmly.

The showman sighed deeply and proceeded to add further notes to the collection on the table.

' Sixty-five, sixty-eight, seventy, seventy-five, there ! ' he ended. ' There, Missus, you'd like a nice fur coat I reckon, an' t' dog's mine, come now.'

The landlady of the Three Harrows tossed her head and laughed scornfully.

' I've got a nice fur coat upstairs, thank you kindly mister, and if I hadn't I shouldn't fancy going about with my dog on my back ! ' She made a royal gesture of dismissal.

There was nothing for it but to gather up the pile of notes, which the disgruntled showman proceeded to do.

And that was the afternoon.

Now it was evening and Magpie was lying in his accustomed place, musing idly on the events of the day, while his Missus regaled the tap-room with a racy account of the attempted ' deal ' of the afternoon. Most of the patrons of the Three Harrows regarded her over their brimming glasses with heavy astonishment, but only one man dared to voice the general air of surprise and disapproval.

' Tha means ter say tha let all that there good brass walk outer the door all on account o' a gert, clumsy, useless brute loike yon ? '

The owner of Magpie and the Three Harrows favoured the intrepid speaker with a withering glance.

' I do that, George Lodge ', she said. ' There's none so many dogs like 'im goin' about ; if it 'ad been a man as I were asked to sell, now, I'd likely 'ave 'ad a bit different tale to tell, but there's no buyers for thee and thy likes, more's the pity— ! '

A clock whirred and struck solemnly a single note. Magpie, out
in the passage, raised his head and listened intently, then
he padded heavily into the tap-room, lifted his
great splotched head and barked loudly
and warningly, once, twice, thrice,
' Time, gentlemen ! '

40

CAUTIOUS OVERTURES

"A poor thing but mine own."

His First Flea

★ ★

THE discovery of baby's first tooth is a great and joyous moment crowded with surprise and triumph. The discovery of Bonzo's first flea is likewise a moment full of surprise, but entirely lacking the joy and triumph of the former discovery.

We are many of us familiar with that painful and astounding sense of shock that comes when we find that Bonzo has possessed himself of a flea, or it may even be fleas. Our astonishment is only equalled by our wrath that so lowly and noisome a creature should have had the hideous effrontery to take up its abode on our dog. While freely admitting the usefulness of most of our dumb brothers and sisters, it is a bit of a poser to find good and sufficient reasons for the existence of fleas. While they, possibly, serve as a source of distraction to a dog, if they are in any numbers (and where there is one flea we can be reasonably sure that it will have a brother or sister or relatives of some kind at a convenient distance) they will not merely distract a dog but drive him to distraction—a very different thing.

But the immediate problem which confronts us is, where could Bonzo have acquired his parasite ? Because Bonzo never does have fleas, and the Smiths' dog never does, nor does the dog of Mrs. Jones, in fact not one of our friends' dogs have fleas ; no friend's dog ever has. But in some mysterious way the miracle has been wrought. Bonzo has a flea.

Of course we have our own dark suspicions which are really more than just surmise. In fact we would almost go so far as to name the dog. Last time Mrs. Jones brought her dog to the house he scratched. It is understood of course that a dog only scratches for one reason— because he has fleas.

Thus the criminal is tracked down, and the next time we are favoured by his presence at our house we look at him narrowly and darkly, keeping our little Bonzo beside us, and as far as possible from the contaminating presence of the stranger. We wait with bated breath for him to start scratching, and the moment he does so we look at each

MISUNDERSTOOD

"Oh for the wings of a dove!"

other with unholy triumph. There ! we know now from whom dear, little Bonzo has acquired his unwelcome guest ; this is very satisfactory so far as it goes. The next step is rather a delicate one—we mean how to convey to Mrs. Jones the distressing news that her little dog, Rags, has—oh whisper it—fleas ? We cannot even break it gently, as it were, and say ' a flea ' because, having, as we know to our cost, already generously parted with at least one to Bonzo, he is still scratching, so we must be brutally truthful and say ' fleas '. We hover round the point over and over again, but cannot manœuvre the conversation to the desired topic.

' Oh—er—how is dear, little Rags ? ' we say, ' he seems a bit fidgety.'

This is pure fantasy on our part, as at the moment Rags is getting down to the heart of things ; why, the dog is simply shouting the news aloud himself. Gazing on Rags's zeal we feel even a slight pity for Rags's mistress.

She goes a little pink and makes a quite ineffective attempt to put a check on Rags's quest.

' Poor little chap ', we murmur, falsely sympathetic, ' he does seem in a bad way.'

Mrs. Jones goes two shades redder and then leans forward apologetically.

' Well, really, as a matter of fact, I found a flea on him this morning.' She pauses dramatically, while we utter vague noises suggestive of surprise and sympathy.

' Yes ', proceeds Mrs. Jones, warming to her work. ' I can't think how he got it because he *never* has them.'

She brings out the old familiar myth with a triumphant air. Then after waiting a little to let this piece of intelligence sink in, she deals the final blow.

' Do you think ', she says, approaching the horrid point delicately, ' that Rags could have got it from your Bonzo ? They were playing together the day before yesterday. I really can't think where else he *can* have got it.' She goes on quite regardless of our shocked feelings. ' If I were you ', she finishes up brightly, ' I should give him ' (our immaculate Bonzo !) ' a good bath with lysol. I've heard it's an excel-

lent thing ; I've not tried it myself because Rags never has fleas ; I
shall have to give it a trial now.'

She puts a dark, sinister emphasis on the last word and
makes an effective exit, accompanied by
Rags and, we hope, this time,
his full comple-
ment.

Rima fetches the
handkerchief

There's something wrong with this bed!

Changing Beds

★ ★

EACH morning between those peculiarly ungodly hours of one and two a.m., when human vitality is said to be at its lowest ebb, I am awakened by scuffling and rummaging sounds from the bed next to mine. Then a series of little thuds, as though bones were being thrown out on to the floor, after which there is a creaking sound followed by a long drawn-out whine.

By this time I am wide awake and, if there is a moon, by raising myself on one elbow I can take a survey of the bed next to mine.

The scene is always the same; the occupant of the bed is sitting bolt upright with his hair standing on end, as often as not one ear tucked inside out, and his whole attitude suggesting that he has ample cause for complaint.

The conversation that follows is something on these lines.

SELF. (*Wearily*) ' Well, what's up ? '

OCCUPANT OF NEXT BED. (*Crossly*) ' There's something wrong with this bed. I've said so before ! '

SELF. (*Yawning*) ' Nonsense, try turning round four times.'

OCCUPANT OF NEXT BED. ' I've done nothing else but turn round.'

SELF. (*With heavy sarcasm*) ' Yes, the bed looks like it. Well, try not turning round at all, and see how that works.'

OCCUPANT OF NEXT BED. ' *All* dogs turn, " and coming back to the main point ", this bed isn't fit for a *cat* to sleep in.'

SELF. (*Gently*) ' Well, but a cat isn't going to sleep in it ; it's *your* bed, you know.'

OCCUPANT OF NEXT BED. (*Impatiently*) ' Well, what are you going to do about it, that's what I want to know ? '

SELF. ' Nothing at this hour, too sleepy ! Night-night.'

(*I turn over and the next minute I feel two paws on the edge of the bed and a wet, determined nose down the back of my neck.*)

OCCUPANT OF NEXT BED. ' I say, I've got an idea ; what about changing beds ? '

45

SELF. (*Firmly*) 'Nothing doing! My bed is quite all right; besides yours is a trifle on the small side for me.'

OCCUPANT OF NEXT BED. (*Licking my ear soothingly*) 'You've got it all wrong, I meant what about *me* changing from *my* bed into *yours*?'

SELF. (*Coldly*) 'It seems to me a poor scheme, but I expect there'll be no peace unless you do; just a minute though, are you quite sure you've no—? Here! Steady on!'

OCCUPANT OF NEXT BED. 'Hello! Sorry, did I put my foot on your face? My mistake! Where's the eiderdown? it's cooler to the skin than blankets.'

(*He arranges the eiderdown to his satisfaction, turns round four times, and drops heavily across my feet. A deep sigh of contentment—silence.*)

" Please are you

my Daddy ? "

CAVE!

Can't you come out?

SLUMBER

The Stop-Gap

His wrong's your wrong and his right's your right,
In season or out of season.
The Thousandth Man.
RUDYARD KIPLING.

★　　　★

THOSE words were written concerning that 'one man in a thousand', for whom, during a lifetime, you may search and never find him, who through thick and thin, in rough water or smooth, will stick by you to the end.

But should the thousandth man never transpire, and sometimes he never does, there is still another able to fill that wonderful niche, one who is ready and eager to give his all of brains, heart and body, and ask nothing of you in return beyond your occasional thought and a little recognition and affection—at your convenience.

This stop-gap for that thousandth man will not mind if you are what the world calls a 'failure' or 'a non-starter'—to him you will be the greatest thing in life—and even if your 'failure' should bring you to the state when your clothes are noticeably old and shabby, he will still be proud to go out with you.

He will always be glad to leave what he is doing and listen to your confidences, and he never listens with 'half an ear' either, or with a bored expression—his whole attention is yours, no matter how dull and meandering your conversation may be.

If you come home tired and people have failed you, 'let you down', or disappointed you, then he is at hand to welcome, restore your self-respect and offer consolation for the backslidings and small disloyalties of those others.

Should you ever chance to stumble off the narrow way demanded by convention, the stop-gap will be waiting to give you, in the eyes of all men, a joyous greeting when your 'friends' are diligently striving to avoid seeing you.

When you're 'down and out' and your sorrow is such that you needs must creep away and hide from 'people', when their spoken

47

sympathy is more than you can bear, then the substitute for that one man in a thousand is there at your side. Not talking and trampling over your still raw and quivering nerves, but there, just to sit beside you, and now and again to touch you in reminder that, no matter though your little world is lying in ruins, no matter that life no longer seems worth the effort of living, there is still something left to you; something that nothing and no one in this world can take from you or spoil, which is yours, and yours alone, while life is in him, and will still be yours beyond—the loyalty of your dog.

FAITH

HOPE

and CHARITY

The black bitch didn't turn her head but continued
to survey the wide lonely stretches of heather

A Couple of Rabbits

★ ★

PICTURE a rather well-constructed scarecrow garbed in a coat several sizes too large for it, green with age and tattered, stained and weathered until it seemed to have acquired a disreputable personality of its own ; surmount this with a small face criss-crossed all over by lines of cunning, with small furtive eyes and sharp questing nose ; stick an old, broad-brimmed green Trilby on top, put a little, evil-smelling, black pipe in its mouth, and you have ' Foxy ' Cobb. There is no need to dwell at length on Foxy's character and accomplishments, beyond the simple statement that, if anyone in the district wanted anything of a dubious nature done in connection with a dog or a horse, they invariably summoned Foxy.

Apart from these gifts, however, which from their very nature had to be kept modestly in the background, Foxy Cobb was quite a clever (if a little crude) veterinary surgeon, one of his favourite remedies for distemper being, if I remember rightly, brewer's barm.

His last but certainly not the least of his accomplishments was one about which Foxy was always rather shy and reticent. He called it being fond of the country and interested in birds and beasts, and posed as a modest but enthusiastic naturalist, but, instead of a camera or butterfly net, Foxy carried in his deep pockets other kinds of nets, and clever little contraptions of wire, and sometimes he carried a couple of ferrets there as well. But his most valuable asset was a black, crossbred, whippet and greyhound bitch, who was what Foxy called a ' reg'lar two-faced 'un '.

When, strolling along the roads, people stopped to speak to Foxy the bitch looked as blank and stupid as one of her breed well could look ; she would stand, forelegs splayed, ears and tail drooping, gazing in a sleepy, lack-lustre sort of way at nothing in particular, so much so that people would sometimes say, ' That don't look like one o' your sort, mister—looks half-asleep to me ', and so forth.

And Foxy Cobb would grin and his small, sly eyes would shift quickly from the black bitch and back again to his questioner, and he would generally reply :

49

'Ay, I can't make much out on 'er, but she's company like, an' the Missus fair dotes on the bitch, you wouldn't believe.'

And well she might, seeing that the bitch provided most of the good meals that Foxy and his Missus ever sat down to, for a quicker and more silent one at ' nipping ' hares and rabbits never lived.

One morning Foxy and his 'two-faced' bitch were idling along down a wall-side that divided a private estate from a wide stretch of moorland. They seemed at the first glance to be merely wandering along enjoying the fresh air ;   only every now and again Foxy, his old black pipe in his mouth, would peer over the wall into the park, and his sharp little eyes would rove eagerly here, there and everywhere, missing nothing furred or feathered that was abroad.   The crossbred bitch paced stealthily at his heels, an attentive, black shadow, picking her way daintily over the sharp, prickly patches where the heather had been burnt off.

Suddenly Foxy halted and peered over the wall again, then he looked down and whispered to the bitch, who slipped over the wall like a streak of lightning, and in less than a minute was back again, a nice young rabbit, three-parts grown, hanging limply from her lean jaws.

Foxy took the warm, furry body and stowed it away in his roomy, left-hand pocket, and they moved on again, at peace with the world, Foxy blowing smoke rings, and the black bitch busy with her own secret reflections.

Before they had gone much farther they met the owner of the park, also out enjoying the fresh air ; he had a gun over his shoulder and carried a plump rabbit in his hand suspended by its hind-legs.   He was quite a good sort of landowner as landowners go, though rather a recent one.   He hailed Foxy genially enough now.

' Morning, Cobb, after my rabbits as usual ? '

Foxy grinned and jerked a contemptuous thumb at the black bitch, who had as usual assumed her ' village idiot ' aspect.

' What, sir, with 'er ?   Not bloomin' likely !   Does she look like it ? I ask yer.'

Foxy laughed raucously, and even the landowner smiled a bit as he regarded the foolish-looking bitch through his monocle.

' Well, now you mention it, Cobb, she doesn't look like being much of an—er—menace to my rabbits.'

50

'Rabbits, is it?' burst out Foxy, fastening on the last word. 'She's that slow, is that there bitch, that if a rabbit was ter pop up under 'er nose, it 'ud 'ave been in its 'ole quite a nice bit afore she'd even 'ave noticed as it were a rabbit; yer can't make nowt of them sort, sir', concluded Foxy mournfully.

'Well, why keep her then?' queried the landowner, with pardonable curiosity.

'It's like this 'ere', Foxy explained. 'My Missus is that set on the bitch I dursent get shut of 'er. Why, if I was to turn up at 'ome wi'out t'bitch she'd 'and me my 'at; you know wot women is?' he struck a friendly and confidential note as though there existed a strong mutual bond between the landowner and himself.

'Well, well,' said the former, 'if that's how it is, you'd better take this one', holding out the rabbit, 'to make up for all those your—er—bitch is too slow to get for you, ha, ha!'

He moved away still chuckling over his little joke, leaving a plump, well-nourished, young rabbit in Foxy's grateful hand. The little man chuckled even more heartily than the landowner, who had missed the real cream of the jest, which lay in a huddled heap in Foxy's deep pocket.

Dog and man went on a little farther, and presently, the sun being very warm, Foxy sat down in the heather, and drawing out number one rabbit laid it tenderly and affectionately down alongside number two. The black bitch sat erect between Foxy's outstretched legs. Gone was her air of blank stupidity, ears cocked alertly to every tiny sound, she scanned the moor for signs of fur or feather with eyes as sharp and keen as Foxy's own.

The little man chuckled softly again, and his lean, twisted, but highly capable fingers caressed the bitch's muscular back and ribs with affectionate pride.

'If I didn't think a lot about yer, Bess', he murmured into one cocked ear, 'I should be real ashamed of yer this mornin' deceivin' a nice, kind gentleman like yon. But you're like all women, you 'as wot they calls a dooal personality, meanin' you aint allus the same, an' thank 'eavin for it', he ended piously.

The black bitch didn't turn her head, but continued to survey the wide lonely stretches of heather.

The Horse-Coper's Lurcher

★　　　★

I HAVE often wondered just why it is that animals so often seem to have the pull over us in dignity of appearance ; why is it that from birth onwards they present such a much more pleasing and dignified presence than do the human species ?

To prove the truth of this, look at any race-course in the country—or any place where people and animals are to be seen together. I think perhaps it is partly the silence of the latter that lends colour to this impression. If they were given the power of speech, they would probably at once become commonplace, and, at times, like ourselves, rather irritating.

In fact, were we to have a record taken of our conversation during one day of our lives, I have no doubt that we should blush for ourselves and very likely, just for a day or two, while the record was still fresh in our minds, those tongues of ours would cease to wag quite so freely.

One of the most striking examples of this dignity of animals as compared with human beings, I saw at a small, old-fashioned horse fair.

The fair, once upon a time quite an important one, but now little more than a collection of crocks and ' down and outs ', takes place annually in June. On the day in question the horses looked an even more dejected lot than usual, except for a few ponies ; they were in the main poor, old slaves that should long, long ago have found their rightful and well-earned rest under the green grass in some quiet field.

They stood in little groups roped together, motionless except for an occasional shifting from one tired, stiff leg on to another equally weary. Their dull eyes looked out with apathy on a world that for them would never be a better or happier one ; they were on the last road of all now, which has never a turning ; it is a long road and a rough, and always at the end, waiting to receive the weary derelicts, is their only remaining friend in an ungrateful world—death.

A little thing I noticed about these old horses, insignificant perhaps, but to me somehow more tragic than anything else—they hadn't the heart even to switch off the flies that swarmed about their heads.

His eyes, as they ranged the noisy crowd, were sad

Seeing the horses which were for sale I was not surprised at the buyers and sellers. The latter were nearly all small, gypsy horse-copers, and the buyers almost without exception were—to give them their unlovely but I think very apt title—' fleshers ', buying up for the overseas trade. It was horribly depressing.

Then I saw the dog. He was stretched out on a small flat cart belonging to one of the gypsy copers, a magnificent specimen of a lurcher, every muscle of his beautiful body looked tense with restrained energy ; he lay, paws stretched out and head, perfectly set on his arched muscular neck, held high, gazing with serene majesty at that crowd of grasping, clamouring, sweating men, shouting and cracking their futile whips in vain efforts to put spurious life into those old horses, who in spite of their sores and blemishes had a certain, sad dignity compared with their owners and purchasers.

The lurcher continued to lie on the old flat cart in majestic calm, his eyes, as they ranged the noisy crowd, were sad, and they had that keen, far-sighted gaze, bequeathed by some royal deer-hound ancestor, that suggests wide moors and windswept heather.

Only a lurcher certainly, but he made an unforgettable picture
of quiet dignity against a background of raucous
voices, reeking greasy clothes, sweating flesh
and beer-sodden bodies created
by the higher animal
—man.

"Hounds please!"

MATERNAL REFLECTIONS

WORDS

"CHORISTER" SINGING

Patrick

★   ★

THE old racing tag ' they go in all shapes ' would seem to apply almost equally well to the Lakeland terrier. I have not seen any two that are in shape and type the least alike, while some vary so much that it is hard to believe that they are even of the same breed.

Possibly this is partly due to the fact that, though an old and valued breed in the Lake District and long renowned for their work amongst the hill foxes, it is only of late years that there has been a standard type.

My most recent experience of a Lakeland is one Patrick, a jaunty little piece of goods, standing on very short legs, and with a long shaggy coat, and a small, grizzled face with the wisest and most knowing expression, I think, I have ever seen on a puppy. Though Patrick is only six months old, in some ways he seems like an upgrown dog; in human form he would probably be an incredibly precocious twelve-year-old schoolboy.

With the exception of one other, Patrick enjoys the distinction of being the only ' alien ' who receives a welcome from my own dog. This can hardly be due to the fact that they are both Lakelands because, seen together, it hardly seems possible ; if Patrick is right then Gamester must be wrong, and vice versa, which is how I prefer to look at it !

In fact they are so unlike that the owner of Patrick enquired the breed of my dog, and appeared dumbfounded when told that he was a Lakeland too.

I wondered if he were dismayed at seeing what, if Providence were kind, young Patrick might develop into, or if he were merely struck dumb with admiration. To be strictly truthful, however, I fear that it was the former emotion that held him speechless.

When I brought Patrick into the house it seemed, at first, as though I were entertaining a small dog angel; his dark, expressive eyes seemed to melt with love, he snuggled close to me, and even left his beloved ball every now and again to jump up on to my knee, put his little paws on my shoulders and demonstrate, with a busy pink tongue, his deep

56

"Patrick, Angel or Devil".

affection for me ; dear little dog, Patrick ! I was charmed with his engaging ways.

Towards the end of the morning I thought I would reward his affection by the presentation of a large meaty bone. His pleasure and gratitude were quite touching, so much so that I wondered if this was the first bone he had ever had.

As I watched him he picked it up and jumped on to the Chesterfield, bone and all—in passing, one can always depend on a lad from Lakeland to look pretty closely after his own comfort. The bone was one of the extra juicy kind, and, after a closer inspection of Patrick's method of handling it, I began to think it would perhaps be better eaten on the hearth-rug.

Without a thought of peril I stepped up to the small, hairy form crouched over its bone, and bent to pick it up, when, with a wicked snarl, Patrick—little dog angel—whipped round with the savage speed of a weasel and snatched, not at the bone, but at the hand that had given it. His eyes gleamed with fury and his little jaws clicked menacingly every time I approached within yards of him.

It appeared that I was having the pleasure of entertaining un-awares, not a little dog angel, but, rather, a small devil, whose main desire in life for the time being seemed to be to bite the hand that fed him.

. . . .

Whatever else differs in the make-up of the Lakeland
terrier, the one ingredient that is never
missing is a generous pinch
of cayenne.

Hounds Are Out

*   *

'LU wind 'im, lads, lu wind 'im !'
Hounds are coming round the bend.

What a grand sight in the first freshness of the morning, with the dew still heavy on the grass, and all around the scent of fresh-cut hay, wild roses, and the strong, heady perfume of the meadow-sweet. Hounds are trying a well-known holt now amongst the roots of an alder. Many an otter has been 'put down' from here in bygone seasons.

Hark to old Carmelite throwing her tongue as she scrapes and tears at the roots; a few of the younger hounds join in excitedly, but the challenge is doubtful, and, after some uncertain whimpers, they leave it reluctantly, and pass on down the shining river winding in and out between its high green banks like a broad ribbon of silver.

Some of the hounds are splashing along in the shallows; as they souse through the gleaming water myriads of drops, diamond-bright in the sunshine, are scattered on either side of the black, tan and pied bodies.

There goes Whynot, the old pure white Welsh foxhound, getting on in years now but still hunting with his old vim. After him come splashing a couple of big, lolloping, rough otter-hounds, Damon and Bowman, tawny-coated, with domed heads, sweeping ears and deeply-sunken eyes, showing the haw like those of a bloodhound.

After them come a score of others, blacks and tans, yellow and dull creamy white, pure bred, rough otter-hounds with a sprinkling of Welsh foxhounds; good workers these last, but one or two of them are perhaps a trifle apt to go away 'mute' with an otter; they lack the music of their rough-coated mates, who throw their tongues much more freely. And what voices those old-fashioned, pure bred otter-hounds have, deep sonorous bell-like tones handed down to them by their bloodhound ancestors. Is there any more heart-stirring sight and sound than a pack of otter-hounds 'swimming the foil' in full cry on a bright June morning? I doubt it.

58

They are still working upstream. Now Coaster on the other side of the river has caught a whiff of the otter in the rough sedges.

' Ough, ough, ough ', and ' Try over, try over ! ' rings out the cheery voice of the master. What a crashing and a splashing as hounds launch out into deep water in response to Coaster's challenge, and cross over to the other side, muzzles just clear of the water, on the alert to sniff the ' ream ' of the otter. There is a deep-throated chorus as the pack confirms old Coaster's find, and a ringing ' Tally ' at the other side of the bend from a blue-coated whip proclaims that he has ' viewed ' the otter. The master blows a long-drawn-out note and is away to the spot where the elusive quarry has been ' Tallied '.

' Hark t'halloa, hark t'halloa ! ' and the hounds are splashing after him with a rousing chorus, as the entrancing ' ream ' is borne to their eager noses over the surface of the water.

Time was when otter-hounds met at dawn, and not so very long ago packs were known to meet at the witching hour of midnight. Now, to meet the requirements of subscribers and landowners, nine or even ten o'clock is usual.

Thrilling times and wonderful hunts they must have had,
those huntsmen and followers of bygone times, who
watched the sun rise over the ghostly, misty
river, and listened to the cry of hounds
and the sweet piercing note of the
horn at break o' day.

Walks

★   ★

TO a dog there are only two kinds of walks ; dog walks and other walks. Knowing this, then it is foolish to fall into that rather common error of assuming that what pleases oneself must of necessity please others ; particularly does this apply in the case of those daily expeditions which we take for the health and pleasure of our dogs and ourselves. It is so easy and pleasant to assume that, when we have to take one of those little shopping trips into the town, Blinkers will derive equal pleasure and satisfaction from the jaunt.

Whereas, if we would only be honest with ourselves, what we really mean is that we don't particularly wish to put on our heavy shoes and go the walk that we *know* Blinkers will enjoy, down by that nice sticky bit of bog, and across the stream where the stepping stones are wobbly, and conspicuous mainly by their absence ; oh ! and through the gorse patch—this is important. It has never yet within memory of dog or man held a rabbit, but one never knows ; anyway Blinkers never does, he just hopes, and he's a wonderfully good hoper.

No, his reproachful eyes tell us that he sees through our miserable, little deception perfectly well, and, as we buckle on collar and leash, his air of patient martyrdom tells us just that little bit more that we don't want to know : that, immediately on our return from the shopping expedition, we shall have to put on our heavy shoes and go for that ' dog walk '.

60

Someone is calling me but—

I'm not going!

THE OLD BEAGLE

The Pensioner

★　　　★

HE was the only hound left in the kennels, and when I went in he was lying down in the far corner of the bench. Just at first I couldn't make out who it was, then he raised his head enquiringly, and I recognised him at once.

It was old Talisman, a favourite of mine, so I went in to have a word with him. I sat down on the bench, and the old chap didn't offer to jump down, he just licked my hands and whimpered a bit, and then lay quietly down again.

These old hounds, what tragic figures they are ! They are not really old, perhaps, as we count the age of an ordinary dog, but when seven hard seasons have gone over his head the average hound is ' done '. His feet have ' dropped '—he's what is known as ' down on his toes ', his teeth are loosening, and sometimes rheumatism has set in. He can no longer gallop, and every successive hunting day sees the sometime leading hound dropping back a little more.

It is a pathetic sight to watch an old hound who has been a ' flyer ' in his day battling to keep up with vigorous third and fourth season hounds, who are just in their prime.

Talisman has been a ' flyer '—no day was ever too long for him, he always came in on his toes, and with his stern gaily carried ; his has been a short life, but a grand one, crowded with zest, speed, and all the joys of the open.

Sitting there with the old beagle's head across my knee, I thought how stupid, and what misplaced kindness, was this idea of ' pensioning off ' a good hound ; to see him each day lose a little more of his vitality, each feeding time watch him come out to take his place at the trough moving just a little more stiffly. On hunting mornings, when hounds turn out of kennel, to see his old eyes light up, as he prepares to turn out with his mates, and then to watch the eager light die out of those eyes, as he slowly turns away and jumps stiffly back on the bench, to sit with lack-lustre gaze, and drooping ears, as he realises that he is not going this time—nor any time, old Talisman, only he doesn't know that

61

yet. He is waiting for the day. Each hunting morning he has the same hope, and each time he is disappointed—his day is past.

The old chap is fast asleep now, his frosty muzzle lying heavily across my knee, and his dark-rimmed eyes with the faint bluish film are shut. Every now and again he whines and his limbs twitch spasmodically. He is living some good hunt over again in his dreams ; he whines excitedly as he works out the line. He shakes all over as he draws closer to his hare.

' Yoi wind him, hark forrard to Talisman ! '

The thrill and the pride and the blood lust are surging through him. *He is living again.*

.   .   .   .

And then comes the note of a horn, just one short, clear note, but enough to call back the old hound's spirit, back from its joyous quest into the poor, useless, crippled body. Hounds are back from hunting.

Talisman wakes up, jumps stiffly down from the bench,
and stands, his stern erect and his muzzle up,
in answer to the call that, until the
last horn of all calls, he will
always answer.

Try over, try over!

Pull Devil, Pull Baker

OTTER HUNTING

She kept her small bristling form
effectively screened from Thatcher's eye

The Last Word

★　　★

THAT Rattle was the best little bitch that ever went into a big
dog otter was well known.   The master knew it, the huntsman, old
Thatcher, and the hounds all knew it too ; many were the otters who
found it out to their cost ; lastly, and worst of all, Rattle herself
knew it.

There is an old saying that the fair sex cannot carry corn, and,
ungallant though it sounds, there would appear to be a bit of truth in it.
It certainly held good in Rattle's case because, as her fame increased,
so, in like measure, did her officiousness and conceit.   Not content
with doing her own important share in the work—going into the otter
and staying up with him until he quitted his damp, dark stronghold—
she began to criticise the work of the hounds, whips, and even the
huntsmen.

All day long she would trot along the river bank, yapping her advice
and opinions in shrill piercing tones that every now and again got
hounds' heads up, an occurrence which, while irritating Thatcher almost beyond endurance, afforded Rattle intense pleasure.

Various members of the field took it in turns to lead her, and one
and all tried their hand—in its most literal sense—at shutting her up,
and one and all failed utterly and ignominiously.   It seemed that
nothing would still that sharp, complaining little voice.

At last, after a more than usually trying day, Thatcher decided to
leave Rattle at home next time and depend on the services of the other
terriers instead.

' There ! ' he said, dropping a wriggling, indignant Rattle into the
kennel which she shared with Sandy and Bluff.   ' You can stay at
'ome termorrer, you noisy little varmint.   Like all the women you be,
none on you knows when to keep your clapper still ! '

Rattle regarded him out of her small, dirt-encrusted, red-rimmed
eyes, and winked ; at least old Thatcher swore afterwards that she
did, and, knowing Rattle, I can well believe it.

The following morning, directly the kennel boy opened the door

63

and hauled out Sandy and Bluff, Rattle slid silently between his legs and made a bee-line for the lorry that did duty as a hound van.

She sprang in and crouched down in the straw at the far end. Presently there was a burst of music, and in poured a crowd of eager, rough-coated, strong-smelling otter-hounds, several of whom trod on the small bristling form at the far end of the lorry as they pushed and jostled for places.

Though Rattle yearned to sink her teeth into the great clumsy things, she actually never said a word, not even when Coaster trod heavily on the most exclusive part of her anatomy—her tail. A cheeky, insignificant little bit of a tail it was, too, but let anyone so much as touch it and Rattle would round on them as quick and cross as a weasel.

But this time, though almost choking with suppressed fury, she managed to remain silent. Crouching between Carmelite and Tester, she kept her small, bristling form effectively screened from Thatcher's eye.

When they arrived at the meet, the hounds tumbled out of the lorry even more eagerly than they had climbed in, accompanied by Sandy and Bluff, two good, hard-working, painstaking little terriers, but, in Rattle's opinion, only poor, mediocre sorts.

She remained in the lorry, crouched close and snug in the straw, only raising her waspish little head when she heard young Bowman throw his tongue excitedly as hounds moved off.

.   .   .   .

'Well, we shall 'ave a bit o' peace to-day, I reckons.' Thatcher spoke with quiet confidence, but, even as the words left his mouth, a piercing chorus of yaps from the opposite bank gave him derisive answer. The voice was the voice of Rattle, who had now joined up, but wisely chosen the opposite bank to that which the huntsman had taken.

With the broad sunshiny river between, she could address him fluently and at length, and from the other side Thatcher regarded her with concentrated bitterness.

'Being a bitch, you would 'ave the last word', he said heavily. 'If the Lord 'ad only done the job ter rights 'E'd 'av made all you females short-tongued 'uns !'

And 'yap, yap, yap' came blithely back across the dancing water.

64

DINNER TIME

Other People's Dogs

★　　　★

WHY is it that other people's dogs, in common with their children, are, always and without exception, less interesting, beautiful and clever than our own ?

The other fellow's dog, more often than not, appears to our critical eyes a dull, ordinary sort of tyke, quite unworthy of the tender care and lavish praise bestowed upon it by its deluded owner.

Is it not a certain and undisputed fact that the moment our friends purchase, adopt, or have thrust upon them, a dog, they at the same time invest in a pair of rose-coloured spectacles, with the aid of which they view the animal for the remainder of its natural life ? Well, this so far as it goes would be all very nice and suitable, particularly so from the dog's point of view, if only they left it at that and were content to regard their dogs in this way themselves, but unfortunately, and here is the rub, they're not ; you or I, or any other unfortunate who happens to drop in must do likewise, and behold their often strange and uncouth pets in exactly the same admiring fashion.

And what irritating little ways those other people's dogs have, faults that would, strangely enough, appear to have passed our own dog over, but how large they loom in the other fellow's.

Take, for example, that pleasant habit of showing his affection by leaping up and planting his paws on one without taking into consideration, firstly, what one is wearing and, secondly, the state of the weather.

In one's own dog this is jolly and companionable, perhaps just a wee bit upsetting on a very wet day, but still very nice and soothing to one's self-esteem. But if Brown's dog also happens to be of the hail-fellow-well-met variety and proceeds to demonstrate on one's recently cleaned suit the depth of his affection then all is changed. ' Badly trained brute ! ' you mutter to yourself (under your breath though). And this without the semblance of a blush on behalf of the little chap at home who in an hour or two, if all goes well, will be performing in an exactly similar way, but with what different results !

You scrape Brown's dog off as quickly as you can. Brown, of

course, never thinks of doing so, he considers that you are being favoured far beyond the deserts of ordinary mortals.

' Funny ', he remarks perhaps just a shade jealously, ' funny how
Roy has taken to you, there are jolly few people he treats like that I
can tell you.'

He pauses here for you to express your gratification in a few well-
chosen, courteous phrases. This, if you are polite but untruthful, you
proceed to do in the breathless intervals of warding off the flattering
attentions of the man's dog.

And then the stories of the exploits of those other people's dogs ;
what a song they make about nothing. How Tricksy insisted on
sharing her mistress's bed, how gallantly Spot attacked and slew a
mouse.

' By jove ', said the owner of a fat and lethargic greyhound when
I met him some little time ago, ' Bessie ', (this being the name of the
unfortunate animal), ' Bessie got a rabbit the other day.' He listened
complacently to the mingled notes of incredulity and astonishment,
and went on to add, ' She sneaked it off the back of a hawker's cart ;
I always knew she'd got brains '. This with a foolish chuckle of
triumph.

On the other hand there is quite a lot of pleasure to be had
in comparing the ridiculous exploits of other people's
dogs with the intelligent ways of ' the dog
that is a dog, if you like ', I mean
the little chap at home.

Borrowed Plumes

★   ★

IT was the day of the Children's Pets Show, and the class in process of being judged was easily the most momentous in the whole show : the ' Class for the Dog with the Prettiest Owner, under Twelve Years '.

A tense silence pervaded the entire show ring ; mothers, fathers, uncles, aunts, brothers and sisters, nurses and friends pressed close together in serried ranks of grim, frowning concentration. It was an anxious time, and the only people who appeared to be enjoying themselves were the eleven small entrants standing in a circle, their faces pink with excitement and showing no slightest trace of uncertainty or doubt. Clearly each one was firmly convinced in her own mind that she was without any question the prettiest there.

The various dogs did not appear to be so optimistic ; they panted, and twisted restlessly on their leashes ; most of them looked rather bored and unhappy. It was the most trying class of all to judge, because, whichever way we made our awards, my fellow judge and I would, in half an hour's time, be the two most unpopular people on the show ground, because there were eleven competitors, and, alas, the prizes were but four.

The feeling of tension deepened, and the sense of impending doom would appear to have descended upon my fellow victim, the other judge, who was huntsman to a neighbouring pack of foxhounds. His usually jolly face looked careworn and anxious. He had helped to judge the ponies, and in a rash moment had consented to assist at this other judging, but I could see that already he was regretting his bravery. Now that he was hemmed in by those rows of pitiless parents, and under the fire of their stern accusing eyes, he had more the appearance of one about to assist at a hanging than to judge at a beauty contest.

All the competitors, with one solitary exception, were beautifully dressed, for the most part in white silks and dainty muslins, all frills and furbelows and pink silk rosebuds. But it was the exception in that dazzling little band that took my eye and held it.

68

A Puppy with a past

THE WEATHER EYE

She was a tall, slim thing with a brown Puck-like face, big, brown eyes and a pointed chin. She had hair as black and shining as the wing of a crow, and it was cut in a straight bang across her forehead, giving her the look of some solemn mediaeval page. She wore a rose-pink cotton frock which was too small for her, and stained in places. At her slim, little sandalled feet crouched her dog, a shaggy-coated, nondescript sheep-dog pup, with eyes just like those of his mistress, as large, liquid and clear as some cool, brown upland burn.

Another point which struck me was the absolute ' oneness ' between this dog and his owner.

You know what I mean ; when one meets a dog out with someone it is generally quite obvious from the dog's demeanour whether that someone is his owner or just merely ' one of the others '. The liquid-eyed sheep-dog was clearly the property of the little girl in the shabby, pink cotton frock, but they were something more than owner and dog—they were two good ' pals '. And the prizes, remember, were to be awarded to the dog with the prettiest owner—that was a point to be remembered.

Looking round the ring I was conscious of a growing suspicion that certain of the dogs parading were *not* the property of the charming little people solemnly walking round in the sunshine. There was a noticeable lack of that subtle something that should, and if the owner is worth anything at all always does, exist between a dog and his or her possessor.

I noticed one small damsel, in particular, who was being towed round the ring by a magnificent lemon and white Borzoi. I was struck, at once, by the absolute lack of connection between the beautiful hound and the small panting figure at the other end of the white buckskin show lead ; but I was doubly convinced when I saw the little procession halt at a certain point in the ring, and a man with ' professional dog-breeder ' written all over him whisper to the little girl, and speak to the dog, whose whole demeanour altered at once.

I took the opportunity to test the truth of my surmise, and was not at all surprised to hear that the Borzoi had been kindly lent for the occasion by ' Uncle Bill '. So far so good ; while my fellow judge was making his selections I amused myself by making a tour of enquiry as

69

to who actually had the privilege of owning the dogs disporting themselves in the ring.

I made the interesting discovery that the smart black and white Dalmatian wearing the silver-plated collar, and being conducted round the ring by the angelic-looking, little girl in white chiffon, belonged not to the small vision in white, but to ' Auntie ' who stood at the ringside proudly watching the progress of her spotted pet as he pranced gaily round the ring. Yet another entrant knew literally nothing about the black cocker spaniel who crouched dismally at her white kid-shod feet, its fringed ears drooping miserably and its large tearful eyes proclaiming to all and sundry that it was that most forlorn of all dogs—a spaniel minus its owner !

I had a shrewd suspicion as to which of the bevy of beauty would be the huntsman's selection. I guessed his choice to be the little mite with the golden curls half hidden under a dainty white bonnet. However, he courteously offered me my choice for the first prize, which I had the pleasure of handing to the pink-frocked owner of the sheep-dog.

The huntsman presented the second award to his small friend of the white bonnet. The third I thought should go, if only ' for valour ', to a pretty child in rather sporting clothes who had spent most of her time in the ring in hauling her large Airedale off the other entrants' dogs. The Airedale was about three sizes larger than his owner, who by the time the awards were made was scarlet in the face, but doubtless the prize more than made up for aching arms and flushed cheeks.

The little girl with the black cocker received the fourth prize at the hands of the huntsman, who, I dare say, felt rather sorry for both.

The last I saw of my first prize winner, the little girl in the stained, pink frock, was the picture of her squatting down alongside her rough-coated friend, and attaching the coveted red card to his collar ; both pairs of brown eyes were shining, and the sheep-dog's pink tongue, which exactly matched the pink frock, was lolling out happily. With pursed red lips and busy fingers, the little girl was carefully parting the shaggy white ruff, in order that the red prize card should show as much as possible.

70

SAM THE SORROWFUL

Some there are
" Who only stand and wait

"I've had my fun anyway!"

THAT PUP

The Best Dog of All

★   ★

THIS book would hardly, I feel, be complete without some reference to the most important dog of all; I mean my own dog, one Gamester.

He has already somehow or other contrived to occupy several pages in the book, but so far I have not alluded to him directly, not because I have nothing to say about him but, somehow, it seemed better form to write about all the other dogs first.

On looking back I find I have already said a few words touching on those misguided people who, in and out of season, sing the praises of their own dogs. I shall have to be very careful.

To describe Gamester—I think the word 'enthusiast' expresses him rather well.

Whatsoever thy paw findeth to do, do it with paws plus teeth. I think Gamester must have imbibed this with his mother's milk, or perhaps it was pinned up in lieu of a text in the kennel; be that as it may, Gamester religiously lives up to it in his daily life.

This is particularly apparent in his treatment of strange dogs whom he happens to meet. Unlike ourselves he scorns polite subterfuge, but goes straight to the point; if he likes them, which is, alas, rather rare, he plays with them deliriously—delirious may sound rather a strange description, but it exactly expresses Gamester's idea of a nice game. But if on the other hand he doesn't care for their appearance, smell or manners, he tells them so, simply and honestly, and, just in case there should be any doubt on the point, he fights them at once.

This method of his has its advantages; it simplifies life certainly—for him, that is—but it can be decidedly embarrassing when he makes these new acquaintances in public places, cafés, shops and so on, because Gamester is entirely deficient in a nice sense of the fitness of things; 'everything at its proper time' has no meaning for him, hence the disadvantages of this sometimes rather charming enthusiasm of his.

When strangers see Gamester for the first time they usually say, 'Oh, what a dear, little face, but, er—*what* is he?'

71

I rather enjoy this because I am perfectly aware of the fact that, in their own minds, these people are quite certain that they are beholding a small mongrel and that I shall presently have to tell them so in a long-winded, apologetic sort of way. While, as it is, I can look them straight in the eyes and proclaim that he is a Lakeland terrier whose family has long assisted the efforts of a well-known and properly accredited pack of otter-hounds ; this little diversion never fails to amuse me because I can watch their incredulity struggling with their polite interest.

I fancy that, to a large number of people, Lakeland terrier is only another name for mongrel terrier. The lad from Lakeland is, as yet, still something of a stranger to the majority of people, and, so far, has not been trimmed and transformed into the orthodox terrier shape ; and long may it be before such a thing comes to pass.

I like their rough, untrimmed, grizzled coats and their lean, wiry conformation ; they show from head to stern that they can and will do their job efficiently, and whether the same can be said of fifty per cent. of terriers on the show bench to-day is a very moot point. But anyone who has watched a Lakeland terrier tackle a big hill fox or bolt an otter, can take off his hat to a ' real game sort '.

But as no rose is said to be without its thorn, one must reluctantly point out the reverse side of the picture and indicate that, along with his fighting spirit and high courage, the Lakeland has a rather peppery temper ; this is not to be wondered at, however, when it is remembered that the various breeds from which the Lakeland terrier has been evolved have each been endowed with a liberal dose of the pepper-pot.

But we seem to have wandered from the point—Gamester's enthusiasms. Another of these is the collecting hobby.

When one gets a new dog, a useful device for gaining his confidence and getting him to ' settle ', is to give him some garment of one's own. anything which one has worn recently oneself, to sleep on for the first night or two. This applies, I take it, principally to up-grown dogs whose affections and habits have been firmly established beforehand.

Having acquired Gamester when he was comparatively young and innocent, at the tender age of three months, the above proceeding didn't seem to me necessary, but it turned out that that was just where

72

Haven't you finished <u>yet</u>?

I was wrong. Gamester felt the need of the good old-fashioned ritual and therefore instituted it for himself, and, with his usual charming enthusiasm, has gone in for it whole-heartedly. Not content with one garment, he always has two or three by him in his various 'resting places' about the house.

Again, a large number of dogs so long as they occupy the same room with the beloved are perfectly satisfied, their simple, humble souls are quite content; not so my dog—I don't say this in any boasting spirit, as it can at times be very inconvenient. Gamester, when I am working, insists on sitting beside me on the table—in this way he can keep a strict eye on what is going forward; failing this he occupies the same chair. I once found him carefully treading about on my dressing-table conducting a little private investigation. The Lakeland is a rare 'lepper' and a high table or anything of that sort has no difficulties for him; in fact, taking him all round, it has been my experience that he is remarkably well equipped for getting his own way in life!

On reading through this, I find that I have done very little except praise my own dog, even if in a sneaking, roundabout way, but still, don't we all do it? After all, these dogs of ours can't blow their own trumpets adequately, therefore the pleasant duty falls upon our willing selves—their owners—whenever a suitable opportunity occurs.

And surely this is only natural when we are all of us secretly convinced that our own dog—be he commoner or nobleman, blue-blooded or mongrel, beautiful or ugly—is the best dog of them all.

And so he is, because when all comes down to all,
whatever his failings, whatever his short-
comings, our dog's our dog
for a' that!

PRINTED IN GREAT BRITAIN
BY ROBERT MACLEHOSE AND CO. LTD
THE UNIVERSITY PRESS, GLASGOW